tivities

▶ THE KEY TO ACTIVE ONLINE LEARNING

GILLY SALMON

**KOGAN
PAGE**

First published in Great Britain and the United States by Kogan Page Limited in 2002
Reprinted in 2003
Reprinted in 2004 by RoutledgeFalmer
2 Park Square, Milton Park,
Abingdon,
Oxon OX14 4RN

Reprinted 2005 (twice), 2006, 2007
Transferred to Digital Printing 2006

RoutledgeFalmer is an imprint of the Taylor & Francis Group, an informa business

British Library Cataloguing in Publication Data

A CIP record for this book is available from the British Library

ISBN 10: 0-7494-3686-7
ISBN 13: 978-0-7494-3686-5

Typeset by JS Typesetting Ltd, Wellingborough, Northants.
Printed in the UK by the MPG Books Group

For Paula

Contents

Preface

How do we learn? How do we acquire knowledge? What are the differences between informal and formal learning? Why is working together so important? Why is activity associated with learning? These questions have challenged educationalists and philosophers throughout the centuries. Such debates resurface each time a new technology for teaching and learning becomes available.

One way of addressing these thorny questions is to explore:

- what works?
- how can teachers and learners use technologies happily?
- how can we create environments to make success more likely?

The pressures at every level of training and education in the 21st century are paradoxical. We must reduce costs, increase student numbers and improve quality. We are moving away from 'factory' education – whether classroom based or distance – towards provision for learning of a more experiential, applied and individual kind. *So, how can we personalize and customize learning and yet make it efficient and effective?*

Along the way, we've seen the somewhat painful birth of the 'virtual university' and its corporate brothers and sisters. As I write, some of the 'hype' around e-learning as the panacea and the trigger for changes in education is dying away. Reports of expensive failures of new forms of educational organizations continue to hit the headlines. Instead of the predicted replacement of education by electronic means, we witness a web of educational providers, using ever more sophisticated networked technologies, constantly repositioning themselves in a slippery market place. Higher and corporate education are seeing the most dramatic challenges and opportunities, but primary and secondary education are gradually digitizing too.

How can we now look beyond the hype and the rhetoric and stimulate achievable worthwhile online learning? I have attempted to offer a way to answer these questions in this book through my research and experience of teaching online. As a result, the book is based on the contentious premise that teaching techniques are more important than 'content' delivery.

My previous book, *E-moderating*, was published in spring 2000. The book offered a description of a five-stage model of teaching and learning online. Many colleagues from around the world told me that the model matched their own experiences or, sometimes, that they wished that they had known about it earlier! I continued to meet people from many disciplines, countries and kinds of education, at online and terrestrial conferences. They explored, critiqued and challenged my ideas. They also told me that they needed specific frameworks that they could easily try out for *themselves*, to help them implement each of the five stages of the model, and to help build their confidence in online learning. Hearing their stories, reading their accounts and exploring their applications has enabled me to build on the model and understand it better. I offer another description of the model in this book.

There is considerable interest, too, in the roles and training of e-moderators, practitioners of a craft still in its infancy. People ask for specific ideas on activities to undertake with learners at each stage of the model, to make e-moderating easier, quicker and more fun in less time. In my own faculty, at the Open University Business School, even with its excellent high-quality learning materials, every tutor is still challenged to make interaction and participation online work really well in the service of learning objectives and outcomes.

I collected evidence about what seemed to be working well, and what did not. I realized that some very simple ideas, using cheap asynchronous bulletin boards, have the greatest, if largely unsung, impact. I started to research processes of promoting participation and active engagement by learners in a more systematic way. Soon afterwards, the key issues came together and the term 'e-tivities' was born. This refers to frameworks for promoting *online* active and interactive learning. From spring 2001, I began to run short online courses using the five-stage model and e-tivities as the basis, with careful feedback and evaluation. Hence this book has arisen from action research.

I know that there is an irony in writing a book about something that can only be tried online. However, some people like books to read on trains and planes, and others feel comforted by print-based resources lying by their keyboards. Throughout the book I've used the 'voices' of the online participants and their e-moderators. I hope you will feel their spirit shine through the pages. I hope that you will see yourselves as action researchers too and potential collaborators. This book will be of particular interest to:

- academics, teachers, course managers, teaching assistants, instructors, trainers or one of the increasing band of e-moderators from many disciplines, from any level of education, within any teaching tradition and in any country – you will be online or wish to 'move online';
- developers and trainers in corporate training and professional associations;
- staff developers and teacher trainers.

I hope there will also be some browsers, lurkers or vicarious learners interested in the book. *E-tivities* will also be useful for:

- software and platform designers and providers;
- computer services and support staff;
- directors, managers and administrators responsible for the provision, evaluation and assessment of online learning in any educational context;
- staff working online in contexts other than teaching and learning – for example, community programmes, e-democracy.

The book is in two main parts. You can read the book in sequence or dip in, as you like. Part I enables you to design and run e-tivities. It explores the five-stage model through the lens of e-tivities. Chapter 3 also offers you the story of one of my e-moderating courses based entirely on e-tivities, and then a framework for creating your own e-tivities. Chapter 3 also provides insight into the roles and skills that e-moderators need to run e-tivities well. Part II is a set of 35 resources for practitioners, which I hope will provide you with support in thinking through, designing, developing and running your e-tivities.

The book will help you think through e-tivities for your topic, your subject, your course, your programme, your teaching practice, your discipline and your learners. This is how we shape the future of active and interactive teaching and learning online, together. Let me know how it goes!

Gilly Salmon
Epping Forest
June 2002

www.e-tivities.com

Acknowledgements

This book has been touched by the experiences of many different people, mainly through their keyboards. Ken Giles, recently retired from the Open University Business School, is always supportive and creative, online and offline. I rely on his enthusiasm, strategic overview and close attention to detail – rare qualities, especially in combination! David Hawkridge's patient critique and insightful comments have been incredibly valuable to me during the development of the book.

Thanks to Rod Angood, who interpreted the experience of participants and e-moderators at each stage of the five-stage model and drew the pictures for Chapter 2.

Very special thanks to the All Things in Moderation Ltd e-convenors, David Shepherd and Val Robertson. Their reflective experiences contributed to many of the resources for practitioners. The 'we' referred to in Chapter 3 is mainly David Shepherd and I.

The representative 'voices' of participants, e-moderators and ideas for e-tivities that appear throughout the book are gleaned from a very wide range of courses. These include the monthly, global Centrinity e-moderating courses from March 2001 to March 2002 and Learning Networks of Maine, United States, in March and April 2002. Other participants are from the Salford and Huddersfield Universities' e-moderating staff-development courses in the UK in February and March 2002, and the EDNA online e-moderating course throughout Australia in January and February 2002. I also learnt a lot from the participants in the face-to-face workshops that I undertook during tours of Australia in 2001.

Thanks to Marie Jasinski and Sivasailam 'Thiagi' Thiagarajan for their discussions with me and their contribution to the resource for practitioners about e-mail games. Thanks to Dr Norah Jones, Project Manager of the E-College at the University of Glamorgan in Wales, for permission to include the project, and to Don Cooper and John Allan of the Open University Business School's Professional Certificate in Management online 'Management Challenge'.

Colleagues from the corporate sector kept my feet on the ground. A special mention to Tony Fiddes of the structured yet creative Qantas College, Adelaide's Mark Keough, and Jake Reynolds of the Cambridge Programme for Industry.

The messages in the 'creative' resources for practitioners are from participants in an online tutor's discussion in the Open University Business School. The extracts are from messages from John Allan, Ian Cooling, Iain Fisher, Steve Gorton, Jane Isaacs, Paul Ketchley and Norman Maxfield (Normax).

Many other colleagues offered me inspiration, suggestions, comments, sources, help, experiences and encouragement. These include Christine Bateman, Curt Bonk, Joanna Bull, Susan Clayton, Linda Creanor, Sean Gammon, Paco Gonzalez, Colin Gray, John Hedberg, Alistair Inglis, Tom Kernan, Bernard Lisewski, Robin Mason, Pat Mela, Mina Panchal, Gerry Prendergast, Garry Putland, Paul Quintas, Gillian Roberts, Greville Rumble, Bill Seretta, David Trevallion, Jeff Waistell, Gerry White, Ann Wilson. Thanks to Dale Sharp and Jason Newington for help with the book's Web site. And, of course, not forgetting Jonathan Simpson of Kogan Page for his continuing commitment, support and patience.

I have put links to many of these people and their organizations on the book's Web site, www.e-tivities.com.

Finally, I thank my faculty, the Open University Business School, for the brilliant opportunities to work online and for leave to think and write away from the everyday excitement and responsibilities.

There were some personal influences too. Any typos belong to my keyboard cat, Lippizaner. Thanks to Keren, Helen and Emily in the Yoga group in Casperia in July 2001. Thanks to Simon and Clare, Scott and Becci, Lauren and Freya and my sister, Jackie, for constant interest and encouragement.

Thanks to my partner Rod and my grown-up-creative children, Glenn, Emily and Paula, for their inspiration, which took the form 'Yeah, great, and. . .' instead of 'What? Not again!' And, of course, for their love and their music.

Note on use of shaded text

Throughout this book, I use real online messages from courses that I design or run as illustrations. I indicate a screen message by shading, as in this paragraph. Messages have had to be pruned to reduce the amount of space they take up in the book, but I have not attempted to correct their grammar or informal language. By the way, looking at selected messages in print after the interactive event makes them seem more organized than they really were. Live e-tivities are likely to be messier!

Part I:

INTRODUCING E-TIVITIES

'E-tivity' is the word I give to a framework for *active and interactive online* learning. E-tivities can be used in many ways but they have some common features:

E-tivities are:

- motivating, engaging and purposeful;
- based on interaction between learners/students/participants, mainly through written message contributions;
- designed and led by an e-moderator;
- asynchronous (they take place over time);
- cheap and easy to run – usually through online bulletin boards, forums or conferences.

Key features of e-tivities include:

- a small piece of information, stimulus or challenge (the 'spark');
- online activity, which includes individual participants posting a contribution;
- an interactive or participative element, such as responding to the postings of others;
- summary, feedback or critique from an e-moderator (the 'plenary');
- all the instructions to take part are available in one online message (the 'invitation').

Chapter 1

E-tivities for active online learning

This book explores e-tivities, the name I give to frameworks for enhancing active and participative online learning by individuals and groups. All the e-tivities that I discuss are based on low-cost computer-mediated environments such as bulletin boards or forums. E-tivities are cheap to create and run. They only require access to the Internet and to a discussion board. Discussion boards are usually text based and asynchronous. They are scalable and customizable.

E-tivities are important for the online learning world because they deploy useful, well-rehearsed principles and pedagogies for learning but focus on their implementation through the best of networked technologies. Regrettably, there is no one obvious and easy route to making online teaching and learning enjoyable and productive for the greatest number at a reasonable cost, but developing and running e-tivities makes the key difference.

There are, of course, many ways to use new technologies for teaching and learning. E-tivities are designed for efficiency, however. They are reusable. Indeed, they improve the more they are employed. They involve other learners and readily available electronic resources. They can be used for participants who never meet or in combination with classroom activities or print-based distance learning. They can form a whole course or programme when sequenced care-fully together or can replace or support all kinds of other learning and teaching methods.

The e-tivities in this book are for everyone. They have attracted the interest of teachers and trainers from many sectors and levels of education. E-tivities can be adapted for use in any discipline and for all topics. They are cheap and they are in the hands of the educators. They are easy to try out and to change.

An e-tivity involves *at least two people* working together in some way, and usually many more. E-tivities take place online. The Web or other resources may be involved but this is usually to provide a stimulus or a start (the 'spark') to the interaction rather than as the focus of the activity. E-tivities are easily accessible as all the instructions to take part are in one message (the 'invitation'). They encourage a very wide variety of different perspectives and ideas. They do not depend on learners being physically in the same place. Indeed, many of the e-tivities, as you will see in Chapter 3, exploit the benefit of participants being in many different locations. E-tivities are available to a wide range of people, and many disabilities are unimportant, or can be assisted through the technologies. See Resources for Practitioners 24 and 25 for more on disabilities.

I refer to all online learners and students by the term 'participants' and their trainers, instructors, facilitators or teachers as 'e-moderators'. These words illustrate the different roles that each adopts online when compared to learning and teaching face to face. The role of the e-moderator is one of process designer and promoter and mediator of the learning, rather than content expert. The e-moderator needs to know enough about the topic to provide the 'spark' for the online interaction and to enable development, pacing and challenge to take place.

E-mail, chat groups, bulletin boards and computer-mediated conferencing were developed to enable interaction between people. If a voice or text message is sent, the writer expects a response from some other person. This key characteristic can be harnessed for the purpose of teaching and learning.

That said, much work has been carried out on the design and application of tools and technologies for learning but only a little practical and useful research has taken place on the promotion of online tutorials led by an e-moderator and involving active learning and group work.

The increasing complexity of online programmes means that simple and powerful technological ideas are becoming more and more complex and require faster and more memory-hungry hardware (Cuban, 2001). By way of contrast, I hope to show you that the technology can promote engagement and activity if it is simply and appropriately used. Recent research has shown that what is important is promoting robust and usable knowledge through engaging learners in authentic tasks and situations (Hung and Wong, 2000).

Combining new ideas about computer-mediated technologies and well-loved theories of learning and teaching results in fantastic possibilities but they need a little human time and energy to get them to work. High-quality interaction, full participation and reflection do not happen simply by providing the technology (Tolmie and Boyle, 2000), hence the need to design e-tivities carefully, to reduce barriers and to enhance the potential of the technology.

Many teachers and trainers at all levels of education are influenced strongly by the way they themselves were taught. Most have not grown up learning to take an active part in remote or scattered groups nor those spanning many different time zones. Many educators miss opportunities for working comfortably and effectively online because they assume that online co-operation and collaboration needs to follow similar patterns to classroom interaction (Ehrmann, 2001). The patterns and processes of e-tivities are different, although they draw on the best traditions of active group learning.

Many students are concerned about working online. They see reduced social contact in learning contexts as a real threat. They are anxious about the lack of stimulus and fun from their 'buddies' and on the potential loss of a special relationship with their teachers, trainers and professors. Somehow, without them, a little magic seems lost! Hence learners need support to develop the skills of working together through text-based media as well as online contact with leaders and teachers. E-tivities are an answer because they focus on fun and on working together online.

Preparing effective online learning materials is an expensive business in terms of both actual costs and opportunity costs. Few academics or teachers have all the necessary skills, or either the time or the desire to acquire them. Usually, teams need to be set up with academics who have subject expertise, creative Web developers, programmers and instructional designers. Quality assurance and evaluation processes are essential too but they add time and require extra effort. Surprisingly, many teaching and learning organizations start by developing resources of this kind as they seem to be the safest 'way in' to e-learning. They find that there are no quick fixes, many expensive experiments, and 'pilots' that fail to lead to 'scaling up'. However, in my view, e-tivities are lower risk, lower cost and a better place to begin.

Resources for Practitioners 35 gives you more of the conceptual background to e-tivities.

When e-learning first started, flexibility and choice for learners were given priority over groups working together. However, this news sent to me from the corporate sector shows that learning cohorts are most important for success.

Stories from the e-tivities front line

Story 1: Learning cohorts for Qantas College Online

In 1996 Qantas introduced Qantas College Online (QCO) to provide flexible training for their 30,000 staff distributed throughout Australia and the rest of the world. We moved to the Internet for training delivery to provide access to training for all staff regardless of where or when they work. We consider flexibility most important. Initially, learners were able to start their courses at any time. There were no discrete learning cohorts and no enforced completion dates.

We found that many participants needed long periods of time to complete their courses, and non-completion rates were high. Feedback from tutors indicated that it was difficult to manage groups of learners with greatly varying starting dates and no fixed completion date. There was little effective online collaboration within groups.

We undertook a major review of QCO in 2000. As a result, we introduced new enrolments processes. Learning groups are now developed based on enrolment within a particular month. For example, all participants enrolling in a course in November are treated as a learning cohort. The learning management system was upgraded to allow tutors and learners to identify and communicate more directly with their learning cohorts. A standard three-month completion time was also placed on learners.

Cohorts working together have proved effective in accommodating the business's requirement for maximum flexibility of training while maintaining educational integrity. Tutors are able to manage learning cohorts effectively. Completion rates and online collaboration between groups have significantly increased.

Tony Fiddes
Manager Strategic HRD
Qantas Airways Ltd

There is strong evidence that communicating through text on screen is a new genre in its own right and that most people are still getting to grips with it. There really are no well-established rules. Behaviour and language online are in transition, despite the codes of practice that are frequently offered for appropriate modes of operating. As shorthand, we can use David Crystal's term 'Netspeak' (Crystal, 2001, p. 170). For e-tivities we try to use Netspeak to provide a clear set of motivating and interesting instructions, which we call the 'invitation'.

By way of illustration, new online participants wrote the following to me about their experiences:

It is a very special and unique experience for me. To send an e-mail to our online conference is like talking (writing) right out in the air – to everyone and no one!? I'm just crawling about online. . . And when I get an answer back. . . I'm amazed! KO

Excuse me where exactly am I? Do I go through a new kind of looking glass into my lecture hall? Why do my words dance as if on a stage? MO

Thank you for the invitation to take part. I know what I'm meant to do, and even who I am meant to do it with. . . but tell me, where's the drinks? PP

> It's fun, it's new. I like being involved. Before, the telephone was the master, now its text on the screen. My own personal access to the world! So much contact, so much at my fingertips. I feel skippy inside. It's so unexpected sometimes. It's cool. PS

Participants who are working in a language other than their own have a particularly sharp learning curve with Netspeak. This participant reported her experience:

> Last year I felt that before I could post anything, it had to be perfect! Then sometimes I was too late, simply because the discussion had moved on. This year, I saw native speakers make mistakes too. They mistype words or they write as they would speak, and then I felt more self-confident! I said to myself, 'It needn't be perfect, why don't you just try and join in?' And this is what I did! Maybe sometimes it was nonsense, but at least I tried, and I think text communication can only work online if you say something and somebody else says, 'yes, but'. . . and then maybe make you think again. So it was also new to me that you can write something and it's still like speaking to somebody, and you can always correct yourself or add things. GB

Writing on screen can be playful, liberating and releasing. Emotions can often surface and be expressed when they could not do so in face-to-face situations. We know that involving emotions helps to promote reflectiveness (Moon, 2002). Online conferencers are often more willing to try things out in a dynamic way than they would be face to face, which means that e-tivities can be more fun and more playful and still promote learning and reflection.

Some people are very interested in comparisons between working online and traditional face-to-face learning. Others want to talk about the differences between online and print-based distance learning.

One thing we do know is that the costs of producing materials for online courses are very high, but savings can be made on 'delivery' (Rumble, 2001). E-tivities help with saving costs in this way because they use existing resources and the participants' exchange of knowledge.

Many traditional teachers are surprised at how much learning can go on through structured online networking. You might be interested in this e-mail I had from a colleague, a very experienced distance learning teacher in the Open University Business School (OUBS). He led a team that produced a residential weekend school; then, with a colleague, he turned to the task of preparing an online equivalent of the residential school. Don told me:

Stories from the e-tivities front line

Story 2: Transforming the group experience

We thought our job was to write the programme for the residential school. If we thought about the online version at all, we saw it as something that would be an imitation of the residential. We never said 'pale imitation', but I sense that the categorization was there in our minds.

How wrong we were. How much the preparation – the design, the reworking of the residential material – and the observation of the online school in action have changed my mind. The online school revealed itself as a remarkable event. As we worked on the design, and as we subsequently observed the virtual exchanges, so the remarkable features of the online environment came into view, one by one.

At residential schools, the contributions by the students are oral, short and immediate. During the sales and marketing role-play exercise, students air their initial thoughts on the task, and the only sources of ideas, concepts and models from the course are the students' own memories. One member typically captures these ideas, in abbreviated form, on a flip chart. By contrast, online, everyone has a full record of everything that has been 'said'. The contributions are considered and thoughtful in a way that is not possible during the face-to-face schools. There is scope for thought-fulness and for reflection.

The role of the face-to-face tutor also differs from the role of e-moderator. At the residential school, the tutor may join a group for a while, sense what's going on and contribute as judgement directs, then leave. The tutor also acts as a 'postperson' – to deliver the handouts! Because the e-moderator hears (reads) everything that is said (written) and can contribute, in an equally permanent fashion, without disturbing the discussion, the online experience challenges this familiar model. A student posts a thoughtful message, which is read not only by the group but by the e-moderator too. Another follows this. The e-moderator acts more as a commentator than a facilitator in such a circumstance. Online, not only does the e-moderator post the handout but he or she can also comment on it – act as a mediator between the content and the learning.

Don Cooper
Open University Business School

Accepting the challenge

The work from which this book derives is very much in the action research tradition. Action research involves the exploration of many aspects of online teaching through research into practice and experience. You can read about my methods in Salmon (2000a) and Salmon (2002a). I have tried as much as possible to weave the principles into practice-based advice and examples.

I see the role of designing and running e-tivities as belonging to the e-moderator (rather than the technical people). I suggest that each e-moderator can have a wonderfully important role in structuring and creating productive e-learning encounters.

To be successful in designing and running e-tivities you will need some passion and commitment. At the moment, working online involves shifting time about and changing patterns of how you work with colleagues and students. It involves setting up a computer and getting the software to work to your satisfaction, which may include going cap in hand to others for help. You may need to rethink your teaching and consider what is really important about the subject matter you want to teach. I hope to shine a light on a pathway for making all this more manageable and productive. It's great fun when it works. It has its own momentum. Just try it – it'll turn you into an action researcher, collaborating with your learners.

Indeed, I think it's time to harness the power of online learning for our purposes. You may think this fanciful but read on and then try it and see. This book is full of the magic of those who have trodden the path just Internet moments before you. Just try it.

Part II of this book extends some practical assistance for you.

Chapter 2 now describes a five-stage model that will help you with developing e-tivities.

Chapter 2

The five-stage framework and e-tivities

For online learning to be successful and happy, participants need to be supported through a structured developmental process. This chapter offers a description of my five-stage model, which can provide a 'scaffold' for a structured and paced programme of e-tivities. 'Scaffolding' means gradually building on participants' previous experience. A structured learning scaffold offers essential support and development to participants at each stage as they build up expertise in learning online. Each stage requires e-tivities of a different nature, as I will outline. First, I will explain the basis of the five-stage model.

Figure 2.1 demonstrates the model of teaching and learning online, researched and developed from scratch based on the experience of early participants in computer-mediated conferencing but subsequently applied to corporate training and across many learning disciplines and for different levels of education and contexts. See chapter 2 of my previous book, *E-moderating,* for more details of the original research into the model (Salmon, 2000a).

In summary, the five-stage model provides an example of how participants can benefit from increasing skill and comfort in working, networking and learning online, and what e-moderators need to do at each stage to help them to achieve this success. The model shows how to motivate online participants, to build learning through appropriate e-tivities and to pace e-learners through programmes of training and development.

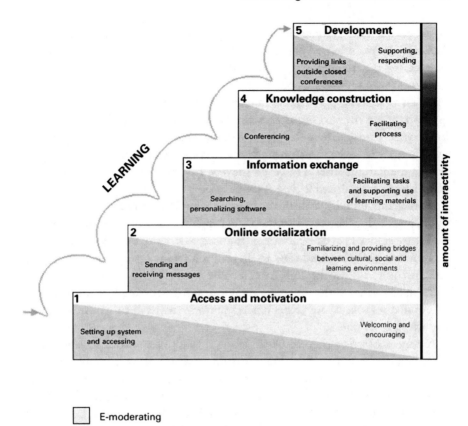

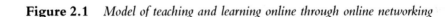

Figure 2.1   *Model of teaching and learning online through online networking*

Individual access and the induction of participants into online learning are essential prerequisites for online conference participation (stage 1, at the base of the flights of steps). Stage 2 involves individual participants establishing their online identities and then finding others with whom to interact. At stage 3, participants engage in mutual exchange of information. Up to and including stage 3, a form of co-operation occurs whereby each person supports the other participants' goals. At stage 4, course-related group discussions develop and the interaction becomes more collaborative. At stage 5, participants look for more benefits from the system to help them achieve personal goals and reflect on the learning processes.

Each stage requires participants to master certain technical skills (shown in the bottom left of each step). Each stage calls for different e-moderating skills (shown on the right top of each step). The 'interactivity bar' running along the right of the flight of steps suggests the intensity of interactivity that you can expect between the participants at each stage. At first, at stage 1, they interact only with one or two others. After stage 2, the numbers of others with whom they interact, and the frequency, gradually increases, although stage 5 often results in a return to more individual pursuits.

Given technical support, good human intervention from an e-moderator, and appropriate e-tivities to promote action and interaction, nearly *all* participants will progress through these stages of use of asynchronous networking opportunities. Stages 3–5 are the more productive and constructive stages for learning and developmental purposes. However, they will work better if participants have taken part in stage 1 and 2 type e-tivities first.

Participants will differ in the amount of time each will need at every stage before progressing. For example, the model applies to all online learning software, but if experienced participants are introduced to online learning platforms that are new to them, they will tend to linger for a while at stages 1 or 2 but then move on quite rapidly through the stages. People are likely to cycle through the model many times as they increase their knowledge and explore knowledge in different domains. More experienced participants will move more rapidly towards stages 4 and 5.

A benefit of using the model to design development processes and build a programme of e-tivities for online learning is that you will know how individuals are likely to exploit the system at each stage and you can thus avoid common pitfalls. The results should be active online learning, good contributions, interaction between participants and increased student satisfaction. E-moderators who understand the model and apply it should enjoy their work more, and spend less time trying to recruit recalcitrant participants and more time designing and running creative e-tivities.

Let me now go into more detail about the stages of the model.

Stage 1: Access and motivation

For e-moderators and participants alike, being able to gain access quickly and easily to your online system is one key issue at stage 1. The other is being motivated to spend time and effort and to keep on returning to take part. There is a complex interplay between the participants' technical access and skills and the motivation to be active online.

E-moderators should not be complacent about entry level skills to online learning. There are still many novices 'out there'. However, what really matters here is acquiring the *emotional and social* capacity to learn with others online. Technical skills can be acquired and disposed of as needs be. Feelings about being unable to take part successfully are more significant than precise technical skills.

Lou at stage 1. Our new online learner, Lou, is experiencing considerable frustration as he tries to log on and take part in his online forum

Access

Let us consider the issue of access to the system first. At this first stage the participants need good, regular access to the online environment, and sufficient knowledge to find the most important parts of it on screen. If they are to be mobilized in their online learning, then they need to know how to actively *take part* and not just to be able to find and read the screen content.

At stage 1 the computer skills of participants and staff will vary enormously. In my view there is little point in doing skills surveys and the like before you start. It's really hard to predict the emotional responses to a piece of technology and how an individual will choose to use it. It is also too simplistic to suggest that we can predict an individual's need and his or her likely use of a particular technology based on indicators such as age or gender.

The efforts of software and system builders to make the use of networked technologies easier create the illusion that technological systems should 'just work!'. We become perplexed when a piece of technology does not behave in the way we expect. Hence most people notice the complexity of the technology only when it goes wrong. At stage 1, most people will not have the understanding to know what part of the system is failing to respond in the way that they expect, nor, in all likelihood, will they have the patience or time to find out. Most people will blame the system, the hardware or the IT people. Some will assume they themselves are incompetent. Participants can become very upset and angry. Handling these feelings and their consequences and continuing to encourage participants to log on is an ongoing challenge for e-moderators and technical support people alike.

Many people will be unfamiliar with the software tools you choose to use. It is important to show participants how to use the software but this needs to be achieved whilst they *are taking part in online e-tivities* that are interesting and relevant to them. It is not a good idea to offer face-to-face sessions to try to instruct new participants in all the features of the platform and then to expect them to be able to take part successfully. Your IT support people will otherwise spend many hours providing assistance, and some people will still fall by the wayside. Participants will also spread the myth that e-learning 'doesn't work'!

E-tivities at this stage therefore need to provide a gentle but interesting introduction to using the technological platform and acknowledgement of the feelings surrounding using technology. Access takes many forms. This participant acknowledges that various forms of help that enabled him to start and encourages him to return:

Dear All. . . my reflections on stage 1. I am really impressed by the technology, having lived on the weak side of the digital divide until four months ago in Africa. The warm welcome was really encouraging: I don't take sugar, but I don't think it was too sugary! It was a good balance between encouragement and 'work': carrot and stick comes to mind! Next, the openness and easy style of 'talking' online has been refreshing. Last, but not least, I am left uncomfortable at my intermittent presence caused by other commitments during this first week – I expect to be better organized after the next week. However, I have learnt already the value of asynchronous discussion. I have been able to follow the conference and its conversations even after extended absence. I may become less reactive in the near future! SD

Motivation

Motivation is an essential element helping participants through the early stages of use of the hardware and software systems and towards engagement and mobilization of learning. It is very important never to assume that the 'joys' of the software and the systems themselves will provide any kind of motivation. Once the technical aspects of taking part online have been overcome, participants will derive some satisfaction from being able to use the software. However, using the software will always remain a 'hygiene' factor – important but not sufficient in itself to create motivation.

Novices tell me:

You need to entice me. What's the added value of my doing this?' BC

I was surprised how difficult it was to send my first message to the conference. Although I consider myself fairly computer literate, I was very scared! What must it be like for people who don't like computers. . . yikes!? However, once you are over the initial hurdle things get much better JL

Using a business acronym, it's all about the WIIFM factor (what's in it for me) MB

I am surprised at how nervous I am in the conference room if I don't recognize any names. I tend to duck out again! JC

This message appeared in a reflections area at stage 1 of a trainee e-moderators' course. It shows that feelings can easily be offended through Netspeak too:

> PS If Carlos reads this, I see in one of your notes you mentioned being accused of being sarcastic. When I look back on this now, it did seem like I'd done this – why didn't you e-mail me to tell me I'd got it wrong? A useful learning point for me about being careful of interpreting intent and then committing it to a message. Sorry, Carlos! BC.

At stage 1, e-moderators should first focus on building e-tivities that enable participants to become involved and contribute and start to develop skills for themselves. Stage 1 e-tivities should directly enable participants to increase their comfort with the use of the technology in an integrated and worthwhile way for them. We have found this more successful than attempting to teach online learning skills or use of a particular platform on their own. Then e-moderators can carry on to provide pathways for the rest of the interactive learning process.

The key is to mobilize participants' understanding about why they are learning, why in this way, as well as what they have to do to take part. Even the most apparently confident individuals need support at the beginning. Later, you need to give constant feedback on how their learning is progressing and suggest what changes they need to make. 'Motivators' should be integrally involved in your e-tivities as part of both the process and the experience. Motivation is not something that you can set out to create on its own.

As an aside, it's clear that negatives along the lines of 'bad dog – no biscuit' are not successful! Nor is it useful to assume that awarding marks for contribution will be enough. Furthermore, it is just *so easy* to demotivate e-learners at this stage as many may believe that they have to get over the hurdle of setting up the computer, of 'meeting' with classmates and exposing their own ignorance. An uninteresting e-tivity or a chance unfortunate remark can be a strong demotivator. For example, a participant who is herself confident and competent in her everyday teaching said:

> When things didn't work as I expected during my first few days in this programme, I became very annoyed, mainly with myself, but also with the software and those who had suggested that I try this experience. The feelings were so strong that they reminded me of when I brought my first baby home from hospital. I had been more than competent previously in teaching and managing a class of 33 six-year-olds. But I couldn't cope with

> one small baby. And suddenly, online, the feelings of being out of control occurred again! Fortunately, three weeks later the feelings are a distant memory, thanks to the technical support and reassurance I've had, but most of all the astonishment of meeting with others online who understand! PS

There are many different ways to promote motivation. You will need to decide clearly how many you can incorporate into your e-tivities at this early stage! One way to consider motivation at stage 1 is in terms of expectancy theory (Feather, 1982; Biggs, 1999b). This theory says that the learning activity must have value to the learner and that the learner must expect to succeed. So clarity of purpose from e-tivity designers and e-moderators is critical from the very beginning. To demonstrate value at stage 1, make it very clear to participants the purpose of your programmes of e-tivities (for them) or how stage 1 links to and integrates with the rest of the learning or networking process, its role in assessed components (tests and assignments) and the amount of time they should allocate to working on it. It is important to clarify the purpose of each e-tivity at the beginning of each invitational message.

It is a great mistake to assume that any participant will want to dedicate hours and hours to online conferences without good reason. Demonstrating how to succeed is harder than it sounds. In different learning and teaching cultures, in different disciplines and at different levels, the meaning of success may vary. So when designing an e-tivity it is important to specify the purpose clearly *and* make it achievable. At stage 1, even simple e-tivities may need a considerable amount of time and support to work well.

Some participants look ahead to the forthcoming e-tivities and consider their workload (they are the exception!):

> The only hard aspect in this programme is the very high number of e-tivities! :-). I have had a look at other sections and. . . every week we will have 7/8 e-tivities! Is this not too hard for people who work all day and have limited time to dedicate to the course? Should I do them all lightly or some in depth? I can't yet decide. Still, you're all here with me (I think). . . BT

This native Swedish speaker, working online in English, expressed how she felt after a week of taking part in an international group:

It's given me a thrill to belong to a group of people from so many countries. A good thing was also the e-convenor's comforting e-mail when I had technical problems and so was late to log in. It was quite stressful to try to catch up with all the activities but I'm glad they weren't difficult questions. I've used all my energy just to get familiar with the software. (I've been very sympathetic with my own students this week when they haven't done what they should.) What surprises me more is that I get so frustrated when using English. There are no problems to understand or make myself understood (I hope) but it's just not me, not my person. I can't make jokes and I can't find the exact words. This is a useful reminder as I've got many students whose first language isn't Swedish. But I'm looking forward to the next session. JG

Some people best respond to 'achievement' motivation. They need tasks that they can reasonably easily achieve – ones that are neither too hard nor too easy (McClelland, 1985). Others will need 'competence' motivation. This refers to participants' belief in their ability to achieve, what (to them) may seem a difficult task. At stage 1, e-tivities need to be easier than at stage 2, stage 2 e-tivities less challenging than stage 3, and so on. This means that the more difficult and demanding e-tivities should be introduced from stages 3 and 4 onwards, and even then gradually.

I feel that to learn this e-learning game one has to approach it somewhat playfully. . . being willing to experiment and make mistakes. . . and not to take oneself too seriously either (imagine a perfectionist like me saying this). This is a real challenge and achievement for me! QH

Expectancy theory suggests two main ways of promoting motivation: 'extrinsic' and 'intrinsic' motivation. Extrinsic motivation includes positive reinforcement and reward (eg a financial incentive) or negative reinforcement (such as punishment). In extrinsic motivation the student focuses on the outcome. With increasing importance being placed on outcomes in learning, especially e-learning, clarity of extrinsic motivators is critically important.

A second kind of expectancy-based motivation is intrinsic. Here the participants learn because they are happy to take part in the activity for its own sake. 'The point is to travel rather than to arrive' (Biggs, 1999a: 60). It is unlikely that most participants other than very experienced e-learners will exhibit high levels of intrinsic motivation with any frequency at stage 1. However, you will observe intrinsic motivators operating successfully at stages 3–5.

Another potential motivator is 'social'. Essentially, participants 'learn to please people whose opinions are important to them' (Biggs, 1999a: 59). Typical examples may be parents, the boss or the e-moderator! This kind of focusing leads to students 'picking out' messages of those people who are important to them online, especially if there are many messages. We noticed this effect in the online course described in Chapter 3, when some people (especially at stages 1 and 2) read my messages before those of the official e-convenors! At stage 1 we think this is a natural effect. Carefully handled, this can be a form of 'modelling', where we copy or adopt the characteristics of good 'role models'. Hence the e-moderator must be an excellent communicator at this stage. That said, in online learning it is important that participants gradually learn to model against other than the e-moderator, but more about that at stage 2.

At first I was a little irritated that our e-convenor didn't directly answer my question about the structure of e-tivities at stage 1 – though she continued to log on. I thought I had been ignored! Then I started to see the way she collected up five different people's messages in a summary. Of course I 'leapt' on this message as soon as I logged on. I was amazed at how she did it. It even included a question to me on whether I could use these ideas. Well I never! PS

Resources for Practitioners 3 offers a summary of advice on motivation.

Arriving

Allow plenty of time for this stage. Participants simply *will not* all log in on the day and at the time that you plan! A few will come a little early and may race ahead. Some will come late. Allow at least a week for everyone to log on, get started and complete the first few e-tivities. You will know this stage is over when the majority of your expected participants are online and the rest are giving 'life got in the way', rather than 'the technology doesn't work' type of excuses. In addition, those who are online will be showing some proficiency, at least in finding where to interact, and in posting messages that go beyond 'Help, where am I?' and 'Why am I here?'

It is very worthwhile trying to get all participants online and frequently visiting before moving on to stage 2. We find that it is very hard for participants to catch up successfully after that time.

Stage 2: Online socialization

At stage 2, you are doing nothing less than creating your own micro-community through active and interactive e-tivities. Whether the community will last a few weeks or a few years, it is a very special learning and teaching opportunity.

In a sense, you create a special little cultural experience *belonging* to *this group* at *this time*. Robin Goodfellow and colleagues call this a virtual 'third culture' (Goodfellow *et al*, 2001). Many participants are very excited at the potential of sharing in the thoughts, experience and work of others but find that it is hard to start. E-tivities help with entry to the third culture.

One participant reported:

> The conference I was involved with before this failed because there was not sufficient common ground between the people, all registered on a doctorate of education programme, to sustain a discussion. Everyone was following their own particular interests. Not everyone participated and postings were sporadic. Some people suggested that we should have all met up, but I don't think this would have helped, in itself. JS

At stage 2 we need to promote webs of trust that do *not* depend on physically meeting. Establishing strong norms based on trust in each other is critically important for the success of later learning in groups and teams (Rossen, 2001). The lack of face-to-face and visual clues in online participation is a key ingredient of success rather than a barrier. If the remoteness and lack of visual clues are handled appropriately they can increase the comfort level of e-moderators and participants alike. Therefore I do not consider that (interactive) e-learning is deficient for teaching and learning. Instead it brings its own special advantages and disadvantages compared to face-to-face working. For example, where comparisons have been made between face-to face and online learning, 'the professors have indicated that they know the distance-learning students better than their counterparts in the physical classroom' (Mills, 2000: 131). So we have an excellent opportunity here to offer real opportunities for cross-cultural working of all kinds, and to understand our students better.

Here is a little illustrative interchange between participants at stage 2. Note the use of questions.

Stage 2. Here we can see Lou setting off in a journey of faith, carrying some baggage. The e-moderator is building the bridges for all the participants

> Another fascination: why can I self-disclose so much to a list of names on my screen? DC
>
> Is that another good question for your PhD work? A hint. . . we are 'a list of names' that can speak and listen in a personal and creative way with each other. And we do, don't we? QH

So, to work together really productively at the later stages, participants need not only to get to know each other's *online* persona and approaches but also to understand each other's intentions, hopes and even dreams. The role of carefully chosen e-tivities at stage 2 is to build bridges between the hopes and the achievement.

> I find the medium very compelling; it is like having a host of new-found friends that one can talk to at any time and who are remarkably interesting and open. The problem is in disciplining oneself to check on a daily basis, which currently I am finding very difficult to achieve. JS

When designing effective e-tivities for stage 2, it helps to consider what it means to enter a new and fresh world with people from a wide variety of backgrounds and perhaps cultures and countries. When asynchronous computer-based learning first started, there was a belief that there would be a strong discontinuity between people's location-based physical selves and their online or virtual personae. However, e-moderators using computer mediation for teaching and learning soon came to realize that online learning groups often can develop their own strong online identity.

I find the ideas of a community of practice are helpful in this context. Wenger tells us that there are three main components of a community of practice: joint enterprise, mutuality and shared repertoire. Joint enterprise means that, at stage 2, you need to help your participants understand the value of working together online and enable them to get to know how they might do this – in particular, how they might each contribute to group working. Mutuality means that the participants get to know each other and gradually come to trust each other. Many people believe this is harder to do online than face to face. However, writing online often involves in-depth sharing of ideas and support. Developing a shared repertoire includes exploring 'language, routines, sensibilities, artefacts, tools, stories, styles' (Wenger, 2000: 229). E-tivities at this stage thus need to directly offer opportunities to share and develop a repertoire for the group. No technology, however sophisticated, will create such a culture. At best it will enable it to foster and grow, once established. Sensitive and appropriate e-tivities and the e-moderator's interventions cause the socialization.

Bear in mind that participants will almost certainly be involved in a variety of communities of learning and practice at the same time. Some of these may be similar in values and beliefs and norms of behaviour to those of your own groups and some may not. Therefore, the e-moderator's responsibility at this stage is to ensure that a compatible and achieving community is built for the purpose that is intended. This is truly a process of socialization, and can leave out those on the margins of understanding, unless e-tivities explicitly ensure inclusion (Lauzon, 2000).

Many of you will e-moderate internationally, or at least across more than one culture. Many others will meet across learning disciplines that are themselves strong and influential cultures in their own right. Others will work across professional divides in 'virtual teams' around a common purpose. The combinations are many and inevitable. To promote groups and achieve much more collaborative learning later on, e-tivities that are explicitly about exploring cultural knowledge are very valuable at this stage, particularly those that explain differences. We have found that e-tivities along these lines – especially those that also give increasing comfort in using the software as well are more useful than trying to teach 'study skills' as such.

See Resources for Practitioners 9 for more about groups.

I think that one of the most important lessons about cross-cultural interaction is that tolerance and effectiveness emerge from greater understanding of multiple perspectives and points of view (Osland and Bird, 2000). So e-tivities at this stage need to concentrate on surfacing and exploring viewpoints. After views and plans are offered, the group can examine them. Where differences are small, agreement can be assumed but there can be little learning unless differences are surfaced and discussed. New understandings arise from exploring different perspectives – although a shared framework of understanding is necessary for this to occur (Tolmie and Boyle, 2000). If differences are too great, the e-tivity is unlikely to get off the ground. So what you're aiming to achieve here is to expose differences enough to result in the creation of new understandings, but within a shared framework of activity so participants are neither under-stimulated nor overwhelmed at any one time.

Both participants and e-moderators should be aware at this stage that their characterizations of other cultures are 'best guesses' (Osland and Bird, 2000). Exploring cultural differences and alternative understandings at this stage is usually undertaken with good humour, though sometimes people can be upset. What you are looking for here is recognition that each individual or group has something unique and special to offer (Goodfellow *et al*, 2001). Later, at stage 4, more of a 'peeling away' of layers can be encouraged.

At stage 2 there are special opportunities to raise awareness of gender and race issues, potential personality conflicts and especially different educational values and expectations. Clearly, this is a major task and not something that can be glossed over in one or two 'introduce yourself here' messages. You can see some examples in Chapter 3 and in Resources for Practitioners 5.

How do you start to know when stage 2 has been achieved? This second stage is over when participants start to share themselves online and the basis for future information exchange and knowledge construction has been laid down. Essentially you are looking for the majority of members to have some under-standing about the group or community's ability to work together online and how they might contribute to learning and development through this medium. They should be interacting with each other and some trust should be starting to build up. They should be sharing stories and ideas and exploring styles and ways of working.

E-moderators should ensure that the social side of conferencing continues to be available for those who want it. Usually this is done by provision of a 'bar' or 'café' area and through special interest conferences. An Oxford Brookes University large-scale study tells us:

> It is important that 'leisure use' of Information and Communication Technology does not become seen as something to be eliminated in the interests of efficiency. In practice, personal and learning uses. . . are impossible to distinguish, and universities should recognise the value of blending the academic with the personal. (Breen *et al*, 2001: 113)

Stage 3: Information exchange

At this stage, information can be exchanged and co-operative tasks can be achieved. The big advantage of asynchronicity is that everyone can explore information at their own pace and react to it before hearing the views and interpretations of others.

Participants' learning requires two kinds of interaction: interaction with the course content and interaction with people, namely the e-moderator(s) and other participants. Whether on campus or in a distance learning programme, content is usually best sent to participants as well-designed and carefully prepared print material or by using videocassettes, CD ROMs and other pre-recorded media. Participants often find that references to course content, including links to online resources such as Web sites, provide useful motivation. However, it's best to resist the temptation to try to present every topic in the syllabus!

Stage 3. Lou is getting used to being online and has started to work with some colleagues

At this stage, participants need knowledge of tools for remote access to information and knowledge of strategies for purposeful information retrieval. However, information in e-tivities should be short and should be there to initiate action and interaction. We call this information the 'spark'. Even at stage 3, participants' efforts in finding and reading masses of information online will divert them from active and interactive learning. You will see from the examples in Chapters 3 and 4 that we use only one or two paragraphs of 'spark' information. You can increase 'coverage' if you need to after your participants have become adept at working online, on time and with each other, when they have arrived at stage 4. At this point, increased content can be added to the e-tivities, if you wish, without it diverting the group too much into reading and not interacting with each other.

At stage 3, participants look to the e-moderators to provide direction through the mass of messages and encouragement to start using the most relevant material. Demands for help can be considerable because the participants' seeking, searching and selection skills may still be low. There can be many queries about where to find one thing or another. Online e-tivities therefore need to be well structured and should always include regular summaries or plenaries. See Resources for Practitioners 29 and 30.

Coming to grips with the nature of asynchronicity can prove very demanding for conference and forum participants. All new online learners and e-moderators have some problems with it during their training (or if you allow them to work untrained directly with participants). There is no quick and easy way around this problem. They really do need to experience it for themselves. For instance, participants 'post' contributions to one conference then immediately read messages from others, or vice versa. A participant might read all his or her unread messages in several conferences and then post several responses and perhaps post some topics to start a new theme. In any conference, this reading and posting of messages by a number of individuals can make the sequencing difficult to follow.

All the messages are available for any participant (or researcher) to view online, so the sequencing of messages, when viewed after an e-tivity is completed, looks rather more ordered than during the build-up. Yet trying to understand them afterwards is rather like following the moves of a chess or bridge game after it is over. When participants start using e-tivities, this apparent confusion causes a wide range of responses. The twists of time and complexity can elicit quite uncomfortable, confused reactions from participants and severe anxiety in a few. Although many people are now familiar with email, they are not used to the complexity of online conferences, bulletin boards or forums. I suggest that good structure, pacing and clear expectations of participants should be provided, not only for the scaffolding process as a whole but for each e-tivity. In addition, the e-moderator, or his or her delegate, should summarize after 10 or 20 messages.

> I realize that I should take full responsibility. I just didn't organize myself to interact more with other participants. (Help! I'm turning into a vicarious learner!) And indeed I have learnt that online learning requires me to be more structured than I had previously thought. RR

There is a paradox. If too many postings occur from participants without acknowledgement or summarizing by the e-moderator, 'lurking' (reading but not posting) develops quickly. It is really important that there is not too much to read or a participant feels that he or she is not part of the interaction. It is common for novice e-moderators to spend huge effort and time in trying to encourage contribution at stages 1 and 2, only to find themselves largely logging on to read their own messages. If e-moderators are too rigorous, they soon burn out! However, by stage 3, all participants should at least be able to access and read the e-tivities, and posting or contribute in some way to most of them.

At this third stage, e-moderators should ensure that e-tivities concentrate on discovering or exploring aspects of information known to participants, or reasonably easily retrieved by them. E-tivities that encourage the presenting and linking of data, analysis and ideas in interesting ways online will stimulate productive information sharing.

Here are some remarks on time from lecturers working through an online course to increase their e-moderating skills:

> Working through this online course has made me realize that e-moderating is not something you can do in small parcels of time (the odd hour between 'real' classes). It needs more attention and thought than that! I need a new kind of discipline. ES

> I have had my ups and downs with the course mostly because of the huge demands on my time (the ironing etc). It has definitely developed my e-moderating skills and knowledge. I have enjoyed meeting colleges online. The demanding workload of a lecturer and my intermittent insomnia often meant that I was one of the people who worked at weird hours (which seems to have upset some). I have learnt a lot from the experience of being an e-student. JW

> My major confession is that I wish that I could have spent more time on the course e-tivities. Due to other teaching commitments it has meant that I have not been able to give it the time it deserved and, because I started

late, I continually felt as if I was playing catch up. It would have been nice to have been one of the leaders in an e-tivity rather than a follower for all of the time. AB

Finally, one thing that I have found 'interesting' throughout this course is the days and times when people log on and do some work! Does the weekend work/early and late times show just how dedicated we all are or how we are all trying to juggle yet another ball in the air! CH

The ideal approach seems to be, as I have discovered, to allocate blocks of time – at least 1 hour – to get into the medium. That kind of time is not always available. This is particularly the case for people like me who are busy running a business and may well be attempting to fit the course 'round the edges'. This means to me that things like size of the discussion group, treatment of late arrivals and/or 'lurkers', archiving, summarizing need to be dealt with very carefully. NB

One of the problem I've had is (and I'm going to try and sort it out this week) is that I log on to read the new messages and then come back later when I've thought of replies. By then everything has moved on. I guess this is driven by a fear. . . wanting to get 'the right answer' and having to spend time on a considered contribution. But I'm beginning to realize that it's the trying out of ideas that's important and that a supportive group is a good place to do that. MD

Stage 3 is over when participants learn how to find and exchange information productively and successfully through e-tivities, and the numbers of people lurking, browsing or 'vicariously learning' are minimal. As you notice that your participants start to challenge the basis of an e-tivity, wish to change it, suggest alternatives to the spark that you have provided, then you will know that they are ready for stage 4! Familiarity with the technology must be achieved by this stage – if not, then it will prove a distraction from the much more demanding e-tivities and relationships that develop at stage 4. Clearly, participants should also understand not only the general dynamics of group working but also how their particular group can operate successfully.

Stage 4: Knowledge construction

By stage 4, participants frequently start to recognize one of the key potentials of text-based asynchronous interaction and take control of their own knowledge construction in new ways.

> I am studying in a kind of hypertext type, which means I get impulses from here or there. I follow maybe a branch, and then I get another trigger, usually from someone (rather than something) else online. I build up a network for myself, instead of following my studies in a linear course that somebody else has designed for me! GB
>
> It is very clear to me that for an e-tivity to be motivating and of use, it needs to be both relevant to the course and the group in terms of the topic *and* it needs to be personally meaningful. Therefore I just can't do this e-tivity as it is suggested here! A way around this issue (after all, you can't please all the people all the time, right) seems to be allowing participants to renegotiate the content of an activity if they feel unhappy with it. (This is exactly what our e-convenors, Gilly and Val, have done with me.) And perhaps also giving a number of choices in terms of content for the same task from the outset. NB

Thinking is clearly the key to making information useful (McDermott, 1999). From this stage onwards, we can develop e-tivities that especially promote the process of actively thinking and interacting with others online. These skills include:

- *critical (analytical)* thinking including judging, evaluating, comparing and contrasting and assessing;
- *creative* – including discovering, inventing, imagining and hypothesizing;
- *practical* thinking including applying, using and practising. (Sternberg, 1999)

Learners build their own internal representations of knowledge, linking it directly to personal experience. This personal knowledge is constantly open to change. Each piece of newly constructed knowledge is actively built on previous knowledge (Lauzon, 2000). Where we seek to engender practical knowledge, we need to draw on e-tivities that enable participants not just to 'cut and paste' best practice from the past to the current situation but also to draw from their own experience. At stage 4, we see participants start to become online *authors*

By stage 4 Lou's group is really constructing knowledge through online interaction, and successfully handling its own group dynamics

rather than transmitters of information. The development of tacit knowledge and its impact on practice can be very strong at this stage.

E-tivities at stage 4 can draw on these ideas. E-tivities at this stage will frequently have discussion or knowledge development aspects at their core. E-tivities can be based on knowledge that ultimately the participants need to structure for themselves. The challenge is to strike a balance between providing too much structure and too little. It's what the participant makes of the e-tivity that is important. E-tivities can be based on sparks or questions that have no obvious right or wrong answers. The e-tivities can offer knowledge building (rather than exchange of information) or a series of ideas or challenges. These issues are likely to be strategic, problem- or practice-based ones. E-tivities that encourage exploration and interpretation of wider issues will hone the skills of operating cross-culturally. E-tivities can start to introduce the idea that there may be multiple answers.

E-moderators have important roles to play at this stage. The best moderators demonstrate online the highest levels of skills related to building and sustaining groups. Feenberg (1989) coined the term 'weaving' to describe the flow of discussion and how it can be pulled together. Weaving together key points from e-tivity responses is a valuable role for the e-moderator, and for helpers or participants as they become more experienced. Everything that has been 'said' is available in the conference texts.

The best e-moderators also summarize from time to time, span wide-ranging views and provide new topics when discussions go off track. They stimulate fresh strands of thought, introduce new themes and suggest alternative approaches. The value of an online discussion can be very high so long as interest and focus last. But there is no need artificially to extend discussions and plenaries. E-moderators need e-tivity closing as well as opening skills! Chapter 3 explores these skills in more detail.

Participants respond differently to knowledge construction processes, and sensitive e-moderator support is important. Adding value to the online networking comes in various ways.

First, the contribution needs to be acknowledged and the contributor 'heard'.

Second, the contributions are available for others to read and they thus become a form of inventory. The e-moderator's role is to enable contributions to be surfaced and used by others. One person may need more time to explore issues, and another may reach conclusions quickly and may become impatient with those who are still thinking. It is important that the e-moderator avoids the temptation to discount experience expressed (or allow other participants to do so) in any way or to counter it and enter into argument. At the point of the ending plenary, the e-moderator can draw on the evidence that is presented to try to explore overall conclusions in the summary.

Third, the e-moderator should comment, at an appropriate moment, on the sufficiency of the data being presented and fourthly to the quality of the argument around it. These ways ensure that the experiences, whilst valued, are not necessarily considered complete on their own. And the e-moderator is thereby modelling ways of exploring and developing arguments.

The dilemma that many e-moderators put to me is when to correct misconceptions apparent from participants' messages. They wish to avoid to 'putting down' participants whilst not allowing incorrect statement to pass by without comment. The key is in summarizing effectively, providing commentary – and removing the original problem message tactfully if really necessary. And e-moderators themselves should always show a little doubt about their own answers and invite further comment. You can see an example in Resources for Practitioners 24.

The role of the e-moderator is, of course, a difficult one to negotiate successfully at this stage. Some trainee e-moderators want to do less:

> I see my future role as an e-moderator in knowledge construction as minimal. If the group are well established by stage 4, anyway. By that I think that the less activity on my part the better. That goes for online group processes, too; I guess that the rules are similar to working with groups face to face. Create a framework, structure, discuss rules (the 'hows'), set the ball rolling and stand back: less is more! DC

Most participants, however, value some structure to diverse knowledge building e-tivities:

> It is really interesting following the different threads that developed in this session. When I read about knowledge construction I thought of it as a mono-construction with a single focus. I felt frustrated that we had so many e-tivities to complete that split our attention but it is by multitasking through the discussions that we have constructed knowledge. Penelope first alerted me to this when she questioned the purpose of the Titanic e-tivity. Then we designed an e-tivity, discussed creative writing, brainstormed questions, replied to another posting and completed a summary. At the same time, we have experienced some of the different ways of online learning. CI

This stage can be considered completed by a joint outcome produced or an independent collaborative e-tivity in evidence. Once you've got participants to this stage, they will have their own sense of time and place and momentum. Another clue is that they can comfortably and supportively challenge and build on each other's contributions. They may be able to move up and down the stages with some ease.

Stage 5: Development

At stage 5, participants can become responsible for their own learning and that of their group. They will start to wish to build on the ideas acquired through the e-tivities and apply them to their individual contexts. At stage 5 the view of online learning can be impressive. By now, both participants and e-moderators will have stopped wondering how they can use online participation and instead become committed and creative.

Frequently, they also become critical and truly self-reflective. It is also at this stage that participants find ways of producing and dealing with humour and the more emotional aspects of writing and interacting. Experienced participants often become most helpful as guides to newcomers to the system.

Metacognitive skills refer to people's understanding and control of their own thinking. If you have engaged your participants carefully and fully at each of the previous four stages, you will be rewarded by explicit evidence of metacognition by stage 5 and be able to promote their skills by developing very challenging e-tivities. Metacognitive *learning* skills focus on what the learners do in new contexts or how they might apply concepts and ideas. These skills can be developed more easily at stage 5, and e-tivities to address them, such as development plans, are valuable.

There is also a crucial role for e-tivities at stage 5 for promoting and enhancing reflection and maximizing the value of the online learning for each participant (Williams *et al*, 2001) and for the group learning experience (Salmon, 2002b).

Moon offers us a useful simple definition of understanding the links between reflection and learning:

Reflection is a form of mental processing – like a form of thinking – that we use to fulfil a purpose or to achieve some anticipated outcome. It is applied to relatively complicated or unstructured ideas for which there is not an obvious solution and is largely based on the further processing of knowledge and understanding and possibly emotions that we already possess. (Moon, 2002: 2)

At stage 5 Lou is confidently setting off towards both assessment and his next course!

In e-tivities you can use the idea of asking participants first of all to recall a familiar experience as a preparation for introducing them to a new one. The idea here is that in attempting to understand a problem or explore a scenario, experiences need to be interrogated and perhaps tested and challenged to avoid the unconscious assumptions that may reduce creativity and flexibility. A key aspect of learning through reflective processes is that each adult learner will have a different ways of dealing with ideas, using perhaps their well-established learning styles.

The results of online e-tivities are available for revisiting and reconsidering in a way that cannot happen with more transient verbal conversation. It is possible to 'rewind' a conversation, to pick out threads and make very direct links between different messages. Emotions can often be spotted, surfaced and expressed that may be passed over in face-to-face situations.

All the e-tivities should indicate why you expect your participants to reflect. I suggest you pose a 'point of learning' reflective question at key times, and also ask participants to look back through the course on a regular basis. Also, suggest at regular intervals that they revisit their own and other people's responses frequently.

> Unlike some, I enjoyed the early stages. Finding out so much about each other helped me feel even more the importance of online socialization. Going back now over the e-tivities that we took part in made me realize how much we came to know each other and how much more productive we were later as a result. It came home to me when AB attended the final validation event and I felt he was an old friend (that is not an ageist remark!). Before our online communications this would not have been the case. NJ

> I've followed the course all the way through and have learnt far more that I had expected. It's looking back over the five-stage scaffold that has helped me to appreciate and differentiate between the different levels of confidence and expertise of the e-students, and the difference between offering 'content' and my growing really virtual expertise! YE

> I have enjoyed this week very much. I really want to say thanks to all of you who encouraged me to do the reflective journal thing instead of continuing to work through the structured e-tivities. It was good to change pace. NH.

> I learnt so much from this group reflection e-tivity. Once or twice it was like being at a mini-roundabout where no one knows whose turn it is and that was OK too. It makes you take more care. HT

Participants learn something new both about themselves and about learning online.

> I also noticed that I was replaying a pattern of mine. I had a bad time with the software, and sent the e-convenor a Very Nasty E-mail. The next day I felt better and apologized – and was annoyed that I was rerunning an old pattern (scream and shout, then repair the damage). Still, now that I know that, I shan't leap to my keyboard to write Nasty Letters so soon in the future: an advantage of e-mails is sleeping on things before clicking on send! DC
>
> Me? I learnt with startling clarity how I stand in my own way, and that I can make it right again. I learnt again how important it is for me to have a large amount of freedom in my learning, and so I think that this is one good method for me. I learnt that I can learn differently. AS

The chief benefit of using the model to design a course with e-tivities is that you know how participants are likely to exploit the system at each stage and you can avoid common pitfalls. If you want to encourage participants to move up through the stages, use careful pacing and timing. See Resources for Practitioners 5, 6 and 13–19. E-moderators also need online training beforehand to develop their skills. See Resources for Practitioners 28.

Chapter 3 provides you with a worked example of one approach to combining and using both e-tivities and the five-stage model, and explores the skills and role of the e-moderator in depth.

Chapter 3

E-tivities in action

This chapter shows the use of the five-stage model as a scaffold and offers a series of simple e-tivities to create an entirely online staff-development programme. It shows how 'one message' e-tivities work in action, how they can be built into a series and the variety of responses that simple, well-constructed e-tivity messages can evoke. It also gives a flavour of what it is like to take part in an online programme based on e-tivities and should inspire you to encourage a similar response in your own participants. Look, throughout, at our attempts to address the 'big three issues': participation, emotions and time. You can also see how my colleagues and I have tried to provide authentic e-tivities – those that have some meaning for the participants' everyday lives and work.

Background

The course runs over five weeks asynchronously, requiring five hours a week online, each week, from its participants. It is aimed at trainers and educators of all kinds and is intended to develop awareness and skills in e-moderating in its participants. In most courses, a copy of my book *E-moderating* is included.

This course, although originally successfully developed using FirstClass software, has already been run on 10 different software platforms, usually on an educational institution's own server and platform. The course is usually offered especially for a university or corporate training department but, in addition, two publicly available courses run every month. These attract a wide variety of participants from all stages and sectors of many education systems and every continent in the world.

We call the trainers in our online courses 'e-convenors'. You will notice that all the e-tivity messages in the course are signed 'e-convenor'. The e-convenor introduces himself or herself by name at the beginning of the course. The course is typically run with around 12 to 20 participants and one e-convenor.

Evaluation of the course takes place through analysis of the 'point of learning' reflections at each of the five stages, together with an exit questionnaire.

Introduction to the course

At stage 1 we offer a very short series of read-only informational messages. These include a welcome from me, a reminder of the conceptual base of the course (the five-stage model), what participants can expect from us and, especially, what participants need to do to take part.

For example, we explore online roles to raise awareness of the different behaviours expected online:

Participants adopt a number of roles in an online staff-development course. As you work through the course, we invite you to explore which ones you are adopting, and when.

Roles include:

- a participant in an online course;
- a developing e-moderator;
- a member of a smaller sub-group of course participants.

They each may have different objectives:

- the participant aims to learn the skills of the e-moderator by doing the e-tivities;
- the e-moderator enables others taking the course to gain from the interactions, and looks towards his or her future practice as an e-moderator;
- the group member aims to work with others to draw key insights from the course and the interaction.

E-convenor

We know that participants often find working asynchronously very difficult to start with. So we try to make our expectations about their participation clear.

Our expectations

We expect you to enjoy this course but we know that you may be pushed for time on occasion. Should this happen, just let me know and I will see how your needs can be accommodated, bearing in mind those of other participants.

We expect you to read all the messages in the sessions, do at least 60 per cent of the e-tivities in each session, and post a reflection at the end of each session. Completion of these requirements will result in access to our special alumni 'footprints' area.

E-convenor

Please make sure that you start the course as early as possible during the first week as it is difficult to catch up reading the contributions that other participants make. If you are likely to be late starting any session please contact me so I can advise. Best wishes

E-convenor

We are clear from the start about what we consider the minimum requirements:

To get a Certificate of Participation at the end of the course we would expect you to:

● participate in discussion with other participants, by undertaking at least 60 per cent of the e-tivities;
● complete and post a reflection message at the end of each session;
● complete the 'Designing E-tivities' e-tivity (session 4);
● complete and submit your personal development plan (session 5);
● complete and return the end of course questionnaire (session 5).

You should be able to work through the first three sessions within five hours, each session to be completed within a week. The fourth and fifth sessions may take a little longer, but will yield added benefit for you.

We welcome any comments that you have at any time and will do our best to respond to them.

E-convenor

Here is our initial message. You will see that we are clear about the scaffolding and the pacing upon which the experience is based.

Course schedule

How the course is organized

The course runs for five weeks, each week being devoted to one stage of Gilly Salmon's five-stage model. Within each stage there will be a number of short 'lessons' for you to complete and you will have an opportunity to practise e-moderating in groups.

Using your time wisely

Please put aside at least five hours each week for the next five weeks, starting now. It will probably work best for you if you log on frequently for about half an hour to one hour a day. As a minimum, please visit and take part in the course at least three times each week. This will help all of you to keep working together. Aim to keep up as far as you can but be sure to start each week on the day designated – see below.

Session:
1.   Access (10–16 March).
2.   Socialization (17–23 March).
3.   Information exchange (24–30 March).
4.   Knowledge construction (31 March–6 April).
5.   Development (7–13 April).

As soon as possible, we ask participants *to do* something.

Your first e-tivity

Purpose: to send your first message – to be seen by all course participants.

Task: spend a few moments thinking about what your first message will be and then click on *arrivals* (in the menu window). Open up the conference there and you will see a message to reply to. Good luck with posting your first message.

Respond: return to the arrivals conference from time to time over the next few days and acknowledge the arrival of others.

When you have done that, return to the course and start *Week 1* to find out what to do next.

E-convenor

This initial e-tivity generates a very wide range of initial responses, each very productive. For example:

Hello everyone, please call me Rudi. I travel a lot and work in different European countries. Today I am at home in Austria. I am currently changing from being a systems engineer to e-learning. Here I am going for my first 'real' e-learning experience. I am very curious and happy to participate. Bye now Rudi

Here I am. . . and I go by Dave. I send greetings from Paradise, aka Santa Barbara, California. I've been teaching online using Web CT so I am intrigued to explore the FirstClass environment. I love to teach in the classroom but I have gained an unexpected respect for the possibilities of online education. . . and am anxious to learn more. Dave.

Hi, I made it! Please call me Lavinia. I have three other FirstClass accounts; I had a little fear that putting in a new setting would somehow eliminate the old ones – so I called Scott at What If. . . and as always, he held my hand through the process.

Hello! I arrived on the heels of a New York blizzard – the winter that we've been waiting for since November. My arrival follows several years of tepid interest in online instruction and with the encouragement of my supervisor at the community college where I've been employed for a decade or so. I would like to be called Marti. I'm excited about my first adventure into online learning.

I am Sophia – a name that is hard to transform into a nickname – much to my lifelong dismay. I've been involved with Distance Education for several years and find it fascinating, rewarding, and admittedly – frustrating at times. I'm interested in Gilly's model, and in what all of you have to contribute to my knowledge and understanding.
Hello E Convenor, David, Dave and Marti!

> I have been facilitating interpersonal communication skills at college in Perth Australia for the past six years and absolutely love it. Two years ago I ventured into online learning whilst doing my Masters degree. I look forward to learning from the experience of all participants. Sandra.

You may need to reassure those who are working in other than their mother tongue:

> Let me tell you I am enjoying this challenge. This online course is somewhat a struggle for me. Not only I have to improve in using Internet resources but also I have to improve my English. My intention is to turn this communication across territorial and cultural boundaries into a rather familiar instrument to learn and teach for me to learn and teach with. But will you understand me? HL
>
> Your English is fine, don't worry too much about spelling and grammar, I'm sure we will all get the sense of what you mean. Best wishes, your E-convenor.

Session 1, stage 1: Access and motivation

At the start of each of the five weekly sessions, we try to make the purpose of the week's work absolutely clear. Here for example is the first message from stage 1:

About session 1

There are eight messages in this session including this one and eight online e-tivities to complete. Please try to complete this session by the end of the week (finish by *16 March*). You can print out a list of the e-tivities for this session from the 'session 1 e-tivities list' message in the *S1 Resources* folder.

This session is about *access and motivation*. We focus on the initial communications, encouraging participation and the value of reflective learning. It involves getting into the course both technically and emotionally as well as being motivated to overcome any problems.

At stage 1 we explore the important differences between messages to a conference (where everyone can see them) and to an individual. We ask participants to practise through an e-tivity. From this point onwards we use a basic structure for e-tivities that becomes rapidly familiar to participants. The structure, as you see, gives a number that includes the stage and the sequence of the e-tivity within that session. In addition the purpose of inviting participants to take part is made clear along with the task and how we expect them to respond to the messages of others.

E-tivity 1.1

Purpose: to practise writing messages.

Task: send a message to *E-tivity 1.1*. Write a sentence or two about what is around you, what you can see outside the window and what you can hear.

Respond: if you see a message where you have something in common.

At this early stage it is important for individuals to relate to a small number of other individuals – perhaps four or five maximum. So we invite participants to take part in one e-tivity for each week based on a smaller group. Each small group is invited to leave its 'footprint' on the e-world. Here is our message to them.

These 'footprints' are for you to leave your group's own unique experiences for others taking future courses. The 'footprints' will help you later to retrace your own learning journey and leave a little pathway for others taking future courses to find. They may be some guidance to help future travellers, a simple thought for them to reflect upon, a quotation that 'says it all!'. Participants who successfully complete the course will have access to our developing Web site where you will be able to see 'footprints' of other groups that come along after yours.

E-tivity 1.2

Purpose: to join one of the groups.

Task: to join one of the groups and post a message to say that you have arrived. Please join the groups so that they have approximately equal numbers. Focus your conversation on the topic of 'access and motivation' in all its forms. By the end of session 1, agree about 50 words on something that you feel is useful to say about session 1 issues.

Respond: to any other messages in the group, to let the others know that you know they have arrived!

Most participants feel comfortable by this stage (two or three days into the course) at getting started on this e-tivity. For example, this participant gets the ball rolling, but restates objectives, uses a little self-disclosure and invites others in. These were messages that got small groups off to a good start:

> Hello, this is Lucy. It seems I am the first to post in Group A! I see our task as collaboratively develop a 50-word statement about some issue(s) related to Session 1 issues. Let's see as others come into this group what might be some shared thoughts about the session. One of the issues is motivation, for me personally. I wonder what the motivation of others in this group is, and whether the first week's sessions have met our expectations? See you soon!

> Hi everyone, hope all is going well with you! As I am the first to post a message here, I thought I would just express some initial thoughts ... What I think is important at stage one is ease of access, clear instructions, logical structure of course, opportunity to express yourself and be a little creative. The trick is working out how to do this! I look forward to brainstorming with our team. ML

At this stage, we borrow from common activities in face-to-face workshops, and invite our participants to expose and share their objectives. We don't like offering this e-tivity first of all, as many individuals are not ready when they're still struggling with the technology. We do not lose an opportunity though to start to introduce the best way of developing 'Netspeak' by also commenting on appropriate ways of writing messages.

Experience and expectations

We would like you to share the online experience you bring to this course and your expectations about taking part. We find the process of posting and sharing a message helps to surface ideas in your own mind and encourages others to develop their thoughts and share them too.

Throughout this course we hope to provide you with ideas and models for use in your own e-moderating work. For example, having posted your ideas and read others about experience and expectations of working online, you might be encouraged to try this e-tivity with your own participants.

E-tivity 1.3

Purpose: to share experience and expectations.

Task: reflect for a few moments on your own online experience and your expectations for this course and post a message to *E-tivity 1.3*.

Really practise being short and succinct. Aim to keep your contributions brief and friendly. No more than a screen full. There is no need to reveal anything you don't wish to. You will see my own message when you enter the conference.

Respond: to the contributions of others taking this course.

In response to the expectations e-tivity, it is extremely common for faculty and trainers to recognize that they need the experience of being an online learner in order to promote their online teaching skills.

To teach online, I think it's essential that you've studied online – empathy is really important along with acquiring a different skills set and developing new work patterns. BL

My student experience of using WebCT was during two of the modules for a course where posting was compulsory and formed part of the assessment. There were also issues about when people posted (did they leave it all till the last week) and about replies (in some cases there was not much discussion of postings). I need to understand more about what was going on there. BT

Through doing this course I hope to gain ideas from other people as to how they see online communication being used in both solely online teaching and to support classroom based sessions. AG

These participants are already skilled at acknowledging and thanking others for their reflections on the messages:

My expectations for this e-moderating course are to improve my online facilitation skills so I can do my job the best I can, and to be able to understand and support the teaching/learning process of our students and faculty. Thanks for the time to reflect on this. LB

My expectations from this course are similar to everyone else's: by being a student and seeing the student end of Blackboard, I should understand their experiences more and develop a better delivery of the course I teach as a consequence (she hopes!). Thanks to everyone for highlighting and reminding me of different perspectives already! DM

This participant is clear from the start what she needs:

As I have had only limited experience in online learning and in e-moderating, I am so looking forward to exchanging ideas and learning from all your experiences. Currently I am teaching 90 per cent of the time face to face and 10 per cent online. I am working towards reversing these percentages. Marion

We believe that the three key big issues of time, participation and emotion must be addressed with potential e-moderators from the very start of their developmental experiences. Hence at stage 1 we offer a gentle e-tivity in these domains – as always, offering a reminder of appropriate brevity and style. This e-tivity results in excellent sharing of Web sites and examples of how interests can be expressed without physically meeting.

E-tivity 1.4

Purpose: to let others online know a little about you.

Task: offer a URL (an Internet site address) that says a little about yourself or your life, a favourite site rather than your own personal site. Add a few lines to explain why you have chosen it. Aim to be brief, aim for a flavour of yourself rather than your life history, and aim for the reader to avoid scrolling. You can prepare it first, offline, in a word processor, if you wish.

Respond: share interests, acknowledge or admire.

At this point, we ask participants to change role and start thinking, not only about their own participation, but how what they have experienced so far might turn into something that would entice their own learners online:

Latecomers (and lurkers!)

It is hard to tell in our online world if people are attending (unlike face-to-face meetings, when it's obvious). In the physical world people can be there and look bored or interested; online they can be interested and undetected!

If they are there but just quiet, they may need some encouragement to get involved. They may simply be at an early stage (in the five-step model) and need to get used to being around. Specific and appropriate e-tivities will help.

Inhabitants of the online world are recognized by the contributions they make. So if someone is late arriving, the e-moderator has to spot and welcome him or her. Take the initiative and be recognized by the contribution you make to latecomers. Show them you care, and make contact! This in turn will encourage their contribution. (There may be someone who has only just arrived in your group!)

Here are some suggestions to entice latecomers or those not contributing. Let them know about:

- benefits (to them) of joining in;
- your support in overcoming any problems they may have;
- how they might contact you;
- what you will do if you don't hear from them (be gentle!).

Here is a challenging e-tivity for you.

E-tivity 1.5

Purpose: to encourage first contributions.

Task: compose a brief message as if to a participant in one of your own courses –
someone who has not yet contributed to your online sessions – and post it to *E-tivity*
1.5. Encourage him or her to take part. Post your message to the course conference,
and ask for responses from others who should assume the role of a 'lurker', 'listener'
or 'browser' (someone who is logging on and reading messages but not contributing).

Respond: to the messages of other participants. If you can, imagine you are in the role
of a 'lurker' on the course and respond in role.

This e-tivity provides good practice in writing encouraging messages, but also
generates debate amongst participants about the reasons for browsing, and
whether lurkers are vicarious learners. A range of solutions are explored and
some excellent 'model' answers are also offered. Participants frequently respond
to each other's messages as if they are recipients who are lurking, and this helps
to give the e-tivity a touch of authenticity.

Some responses are chatty, others more formal. Some address the individual
directly, some explore group reactions.

Hi Karen, I see you're online too. Welcome to our online conference. If
you browse through the subjects in the conference you'll see that there are
already interesting and inspiring discussions going on. Why not post one
message today? We all would appreciate if you would join in and let us
know your point of view. If you go to the 'Arrivals' conference you'll get
an overview about the other participants online – they are all very friendly.
If you have technical problems the helpdesk number is. . . ML

Sandy! Are you out there, Sandy? Are you looking in but not talking? It's
a little hard to tell in virtual space. I'm just checking in to see if you are
OK. We haven't heard from you in a while and we are missing your
wonderful insights into our conversations. Let me know if there is anything
I can do to help. You can call me at xxx-xxxx. I hope to hear from you
soon. DP

Hello, Carlos. I can see that you've stopped by the conferences and read a few postings in the past week. I hope you've found some interesting messages. Our learning set relies on the participation of everyone. Your viewpoint is as valuable as those you've read in the conferences. Please post a message the next time you log on. If you would like to post privately to me, you may do so by replying to this message. I am very interested in your apparent cautiousness in approaching the e-tivities that we began last week. MM

Well Athena Group 2, 9 out of the 12 of you have responded to the Blue Water e-tivity, with Cherry posting 16 messages and Peter 10. Anton and Sally have read everything but not posted yet. Suggest we all have a try and invite them in before Sunday's deadline! We need to get them in before we can move on. Who can help? E-mod JM

At the end of the first week of the course, we offer the first reflections e-tivity. We think it's critically important to establish the habit of reflections from the earliest possible moment.

Reflections and ripples on your pond

The word 'reflection' means to bend or turn backwards. Of course, it is commonly used to mean the reflection of light against an object such as a mirror. Sometimes reflection provides amazing and beautiful images, such as trees in a river, mountains in a lake, clouds on the ocean. Sometimes these are clear; sometimes they appear to be dynamic and rippling in the water.

In human terms, this means reflecting oneself, or other people, as if viewed through a looking glass. Revisiting images of a time past, such as pictures of childhood events, often offers new insights. Reflection of this kind has always been thought of as important to learning and development.

Now some people think that reviewing our own, and other people's, thoughts and ideas written in messages and on a computer screen provides a kind of image, ripe for reflecting. And sometimes what we 'see' is a little different or even surprising!

We believe it is valuable to provide opportunity for our participants to reflect, and to share and discuss their reflections. Our own ideas can be confirmed as others acknowledge our contributions or make similar ones. New ideas can be explored as others suggest to us fresh lines of approach. By sharing, we can find kindred spirits to communicate with later about further issues as they arise. We expand our knowledge, grow more confident and build our networks.

E-tivity 1.7: Session 1 reflection

Purpose: to reflect on how your own experience will help you to provide a better experience for those whom you will e-moderate.

Task: put a short note into the *S1 Reflections* conference about your thoughts at the end of this first session, sharing with others the things that you have found to be useful, and those things that have been a little harder to do than you expected.

Respond: to one reflection by another participant that helps you.

Reflections on both access and motivation go well beyond using the technology, as you see below. Time, feelings, skills development and 'who is here with me?' feature very strongly in stage 1 reflections. Some participants start the comparisons with more familiar face-to-face learning experiences. Some are tempted to print out the e-tivities. Nearly all participants are hungry for feedback from both other participants and from the e-convenor. A significant minority is already thinking about how to apply their learning to their own online courses.

I have really enjoyed taking part in the course. The momentum is fast (although sometimes too fast for me) and I have found that it is a really active learning experience. I have really engaged in the course. I would like to do other courses like this. . . rushing back. . . PP

More to it than meets the eye. . . I think that about sums up my feeling at the end of week one. I seem to have been through all sorts of feelings about the online environment (generally very positive, but overwhelmed by it at times). GS

Things that boosted my confidence were spotting familiar territory and having other students around who were proactive. Good messages here for when I set up early activities as part of icebreakers or course material. I learnt to use topics or activities that lots of people could hook into. PP

I was interested to see that quite a few people didn't feel they had had enough interactions with others. I was only really expecting to interact with one or two other people in the first week, although we all become familiar with the group in a passive way. When you arrive on a face-to-face course (particularly if you only do one hour a day), to start with I reckon you only really talk in depth with the person sitting next to you or some one you have met before and have obvious common interests. Why should this be different online? MJ

It was amazing to learn about people from their arrivals messages. Somebody from Los Angeles, the other one from Snowdon (which country is this?) and the third one from Cape Town and now living in Asia. From my point of view, those who are more 'subjective' – tend to reveal their feelings more (than the people who state their goals or objectives) – are much more interesting in this online medium. However it's not evident the kind of online courses these people are following. Surely it does not seem to be the EM010 I am following myself. HL

I felt that session one provided easy and non-threatening opportunities to become familiar with other participants on the course and to communicate and share ideas and expectations. I needed to become familiar with the FirstClass environment and orientate myself to learning in an asynchronous mode and felt that session one made this possible. My challenge was to become confident with the new environment and it was nice not to be overwhelmed by new and heavy concepts. EI

Would agree with other people's comments by and large. Found initial engagement very frustrating and daunting as platform takes quite a bit of getting used to. Did however really enjoy 'chat' with Harriet earlier. Do find the number of discussions difficult to keep track of and very tempted to print things out. The summary under e-tivities is however good but who decides the content here? WW

Really enjoying the course but very conscious of how far away from this model I am when running own online programmes. Desperately trying to implement ideas, as pragmatic style on overload. LS

Super to receive positive comments back from the E convenor (thanks Val!) they made me feel part of what's going on. JC

The good thing about the sectioning of e-tivities is that it provides structure, and builds confidence. Less good is not sure what I've learnt! Still reflecting. . . takes a deal of time to orientate! PA

Invitations need to be oh so clear. Was confused re message 8 in instruction section, not clarified till found, b.y what felt like accident, the message in reflections conference. MB

After the first week I am feeling very positive about this course. I seem to be learning a lot from how this course is structured (in small chunks, with related activities), and the way that the e-convenors work to get us to build on our initial comments. That way everyone's experience and thoughts can be drawn out, and everyone feels valued. It's like a 'snow-balling process'. It's been a revelation just how much e-moderators need to intervene, keep an eye on who's not contributing, and draw participants in; I can see where real skills come in. TK

Looking forward to the break – coffee anyone? JC

I realize I'm feeling quite exhausted by all this virtual interaction (I've had a busy week of virtual interaction in other contexts too). It's a long time since I've 'met' so many new people in a week! On a more serious note, it's made me reflect on how it's easy as an e-moderator to worry that non-interaction by a student signifies a problem – it might not, they might just want time out from the relentless communication! JH

Session 2, stage 2: Socialization

At stage 2 we concentrate on enabling *online* socialization of all participants with a view to mobilizing them to visit again frequently. These approaches work just as well for our remotely located participants on 'global' courses as for lecturers based physically on the same campus or area. You see evaluation of both kinds of courses at the end of this chapter. We aim, either way, to build trust that is *not* based on face-to-face meetings. Instead, as you will see, we try to address with the critical issues of participation, emotions and time throughout the e-tivities.

Asynchronous working

Here we explore the skills of online socialization in eight messages and eight e-tivities. Our online world can feel strange or alien, so it is especially important to give people time and support to adjust. In addition, each new online group needs to establish effective working for itself. We think that if you spend a little time and energy at this stage, the participation will be much better later on when less e-moderation will be needed.

Here is an exercise we run to give participants an exploration of the asynchronous environment.

Imagine being in a room with other people, every one armed with a pad of Post-it notes and a pen. There is a wall with spaces for each person with their name on it (let's call it a mailbox) and a large space on the wall called a conference. Notes can be placed in the conference space where everyone can read them and in individuals' private mailboxes. The only way of communicating is via placing Post-it notes on the conference wall or in mailboxes. No one must talk to each other. (We try to stop any body language, but this is really hard to achieve! Participants can be very inventive!)

Many participants in this activity become very frustrated as their communication is ignored and they fail to get a reply. Some can become really annoyed if other people's messages are replied to before theirs!

The key issue is that people want a response. Silence is deafening!

E-tivity 2.1

Purpose: getting the feel of online working.

Task: try this exercise (about 30 minutes is enough) with a small face-to-face group. If you can only find one person, it is worth a try. Report back on how you and colleagues felt about it; post your report to *E-tivity 2.1*.

Respond: to the messages that you find interesting.

I tried this exercise. It is a very good and opening exercise. By the word opening, I mean that you have a direct feeling if your note/letter/argument is overlooked or no one answers or respond to it. You sit there, you watch others read your message, they read another message or two, and in your thoughts you hope and expect some reaction. If you get the reaction you can act again, but if you do not get anything, then it gets really hard not to say anything or put an arm in the air waving 'Hi here I am. I've said something too, you know!' OB

Read this e-tivity this afternoon, so took advantage of the fact that my sister's five lads (aged 4 to 11) were on half term. Went round and told them the plot. I just sat and observed. The four-year-old can't write really so drew pictures – the others didn't respond and he gave up after two drawings. The two oldest (9 and 11) were responding quite actively to one another – they're best of friends and on the same wavelength! They started to communicate with the middle lad (7) eventually but only sporadically. The next to youngest (6) kept muttering because his contributions were going unanswered. Walking home and reflecting before coming onto the board, I tried to make sense of it. The frustration of making a contribution and it not being read; the gelling of some members who might seek to exclude others; the different levels of learning ability. It did make me wonder if before placing students into e-tivity groups whether consideration of possible group dynamics should be taken into account. Not explored this fully yet, but really got me thinking! JF

At this point, we move participants back into the online world. We believe it is important to introduce an exploration of the thorny issue of the experience of time online at this stage.

Asynchronous working

Interacting with others without being in the same place and the same time requires a change in perspective as you have found already. In these next few messages and corresponding e-tivities, see if you can develop strategies for using your own time.

People may be online just for a short period or may only arrive occasionally; they may linger there, or not come at all; and they may even spend all day there.

A regular stage of activity pacing entices people into your online world and encourages them to pop in often to see what is going on. Each person develops a kind of rhythm of his or her own.

E-tivity 2.4

Purpose: to contribute to an enticing stage of activity.

Task: send a postcard to *E-tivity 2.4* saying something of interest that is going on in your part of the world. Keep it brief, no more than you would write on a postcard. You may say something about your favourite food – what you can see from your window – something you have discovered recently on the Internet.

Respond: look through other people's contributions (come back on another visit if necessary). Spot someone who has something in common with you and someone who has a difference and comment on both.

As you can imagine, this e-tivity provokes some fascinating contributions and gets the socialization process off to a good start. Typically, people explain their physical surroundings. We find that asking people to describe their physical environments helps to provide a touch of 'reality' and interest. It also helps each person to remember the other. Here are just a few examples:

Hi everyone, I am sitting in my study (at my computer!), having just come in from several hours of burning brush at the front of my house. My study is filled with books, miscellaneous papers, computer 'stuff', and photographs of my family. I live in a rural area of mountains, and from my window I can look out at a stand of towering pine trees and the smoke of what is left of the fire. I can still smell the wood smoke on my clothes and my body is comfortably tired. I hear the hum of electronics and the water in my goldfish tank bubbling in another room (it needs more water). It's good to be here. SH

Night has finally come to Canada and my household has settled enough for me to do some work. Daylight saving time provides us daylight until late in the evening, which really makes it difficult at times to find time to work at home. I'm sitting in my study upstairs and if it were light enough I would have a beautiful view of dogwood trees in full bloom against a backdrop of fragrant evergreens. Beyond the woods, however, is a new five-lane road with all the traffic noise. Fortunately the woods block much of that. I'm looking forward to getting to know and work with each of you. MA

Hi, everyone, mostly I am working at home where I have a view to our backyard. It is covered with last autumn's leaves and there is some snow in places. There are odd bird couples seeking suitable nests, the spring is definitely on its way. My study and the room next door are covered with books and CDs. Our cats (three of them) occasionally help me when I write on the computer. All mistakes are their fault! Of course I use my office at the Polytechnic every now and then. It is in the main complex of the Polytechnic, just behind the main building. My office is somewhat barren and untidy and I should definitely do something about it. KL

And a response:

> E convenor and everyone, out there, in here! Yes, all these descriptions of
> sights, sounds and temperatures are great fun to read but they make me
> want to ask more and more questions. It's amazing that we all come from
> many parts of the world, and yet we all want to be better e-moderators!
> Still clearly we have lots of interests in common. . . walking, dogs, children,
> music, as well. . . PP

It is only at this point in the course (10 days or so into it) that we ask participants
to post up their résumés. We give instructions on how to read the résumés of
others and how to post their own in the software in use. At the same time, we
take the opportunity to give a little more information about time and participation.

Getting to know others online

You may not, at the moment, remember who has arrived and what their names are.
In the online environment messages tend to have a short life; they may be summarized,
they may be deleted. Participants may join as the course officially starts, some may
be late, and others may be very late. So it is helpful to place some information about
yourself in a place that is not subject to rapid change. It helps with the 'socialization'
of the group.

In FirstClass there is a facility to post your résumé where it is easily accessed. You
can update it from time to time as you grow in experience (you can add that you have
taken part in this course!). Others can remind themselves about what you have to
offer as their needs change.

At this point we start to introduce slightly more substantive principles for online
working, and authentic activities for participants to respond to. Here is one
example:

Principles of online communication

1. Don't assume that your participants know much about *communicating* via
    computers, sending mail, contributing in conferences, etc. Let them surprise you!
2. Remember in any face-to-face group some people will always need encourage-
    ment to contribute. Others will want to hog the airspace, too. In our online world
    the former group are invisible!

3. It takes time and (good) experience to get used to communicating and learning online – even those who are highly IT literate. Twice as long as your most pessimistic guess?
4. Many will think e-moderators are blessed with superhuman powers to read minds without their even logging on! It is sometimes helpful to disclose your own weaknesses so others know what you might find difficult. A human fragility in an online world.

Principles to hold at the front of your mind when e-moderating

1. Acknowledge and appreciate participants' contributions. They may have laboured for hours to get a simple 'Hello!' onto the conference. A little praise goes a long way.
2. Be welcoming. On a visit to a physician, it is much nicer when they pop out and invite you in, rather than pressing a buzzer and shouting 'Next'.
3. If you disagree with a participant, restate his or her point, to acknowledge it, and then state your view. Focus on disagreeing over or building on the statements (rather than attacking the participant). Always aim to maintain the person's self-esteem.
4. Speak from your own perspective (or from someone else's, stating whose). Assertions tend to raise hackles and lead to cyberspace wars. Try to avoid being absolute about anything!
5. Finish your message with an open question – even a request for confirmation or other views will help a lot.

E-tivity 2.5

Purpose: to practise responding encouragingly.

Task: read these short messages and prepare a response to each.

a) It's taken me two hours to get into this &*$£"!! conference! Sajid

b) Hello! Have you got this message? Monica

c) I think this environment is absolutely brilliant. I've been online since 1991 and I'm still amazed at what can be done. My dog's got her own Web site. Everyone should have free access. . . [and so on and on for four screenfuls]. Is there anyone there? Yours B.

Send a single message to *E-tivity 2.5* suggesting your responses.

Respond: if you wish, after you have posted your own responses, look at other people's messages and think how you'd feel if you were in receipt of them.

We find that responding to the angry, timid, expansive as archetypes, in itself also produces a huge amount of discussions, support and development. Here is one participant's summary of her group's work on this e-tivity:

> The group's posts showed a fairly uniform and very supportive response to Monica's plea for a reply to confirm she was online and in the forum.
>
> The reaction to B's post were mixed – some suggesting that they would recommend shorter posts to B, others ignoring the length of his post and seeking to 'use' B to mentor the newer, less confident forum members. Others just grabbed an element of his long post and asked further questions about it as though length was not a problem for everybody. There were several suggestions that issues of online etiquette or protocols should be posted as guidelines at the start of the forum so as to avoid the problem of length and/or flaming, etc.
>
> Sajid's comment attracted quite a stronger response, with a mixture of our group suggesting that the rudeness of the post needed either a post to the group or at least a private e-mail to Sajid about aggression and forum etiquette. Several members also suggested that putting forum protocols at the start of the forum could avoid this sort of online behaviour developing. Who votes for this?
> 1) Long comments take a while to read but sometimes (not always) include depth of reflection on complex issues; and
> 2) What is the place of culture in language usage? Does Sajid understand that he may offend some people with his response? LC

In another group, some used a little humour in response to 'B'.

> Hi B. This is Lauretta, the e-convenor. I am really pleased that you are enjoying this online environment. Sounds like you have lots of experience. Could you share your dog's Web site? I am a total dog lover. Woof, Woof. L

And similarly to Sajid:

> WOW! Sajid, you've said what we have all thought at one time or another. Have you figured out what you were doing that wasn't helping you to get to where you wanted to be? Try backing out and coming in again, and then post another message to the conference so that I know you've got it figured out!
>
>   Congratulations on your <painful> arrival! L

Similarly, the next e-tivity is also very rich in its responses.

Replying

Timeliness in replying to messages is critical. If, as e-moderators, we are too quick in responding, we may find we are in online dialogue with ourselves! We can choose *when* we respond to conference messages. Sometimes we might want to respond immediately, sometimes reflect first, sometimes we may wish to avoid intervening at that moment. While we are deciding, though, more messages might appear.

Here are some options about when to reply:

- Reply immediately on reading (this may be several days after the message was sent).
- Acknowledge immediately and reply later (don't forget make a note somewhere).
- Ignore temporarily (others may reply or build on messages before you do).
- Ignore completely (not recommended as an encouraging strategy).

You have options of routes too:

- Post to the conference (where everyone can see your response).
- E-mail to the individual's private mailbox (only the individual sees this, and no one else knows you have responded).
- Telephone (this is OK if appropriate).
- Face to face if you normally meet them this way (as for the first two points above, no one else knows you have responded).

Do you have other strategies?

E-tivity 2.6

Purpose: to write encouraging replies.

Task: consider the following e-mail, which might appear in your conference:

'I am really fed up with the people in this conference who spend their time looking in on those of us who are doing all the work. If this keeps on – I'm off! Andy Lurquer'

What would you do? Describe your approach and place a message in the *E-tivity 2.6.*

Respond: look at the messages of others to Andy and consider how you would feel if you were in receipt of them. E-convenor

---

Here is a summary, offered by one participant, of her group's responses to the lurker e-tivity:

Well done, all of you, for such an overall comprehensive response to our friend Andy Lurquer's outburst! The following issues were identified collectively:

1. inappropriate use of language;
2. how to deal with outbursts of anger/frustration;
3. lurkers – a role/burden;
4. non-active participation.

Solutions:
The individual responses showed many appropriate ways Andy could be handled. Overall the consensus seemed to be:

1. Inappropriate language is removed from posting and Andy reminded that such use is not appropriate in a public forum. This was generally done through a conference message although some chose to deal with this issue through a private e-mail.
2. Andy's feelings behind the outburst were acknowledged and as well, Andy was thanked for his contributions so far and encouraged to continue his valuable input.
3. In general, issues around lurking were dealt with through a short statement of explanation from the e-moderator about why and when

> lurking is appropriate. In many cases a discussion around lurking was encouraged and instigated.
> 4. Encouraging the non-participants to be more active was mainly handled either through a direct friendly challenge via a conference message or through a general notice reminding all participants of the course expectations.
>
> All responses made interesting reading and added positively to the collective thinking. Will this impact on the way we do things in future? MM

We know that there is a wide range of emotion associated with working online. We believe that getting to grips with the emotional aspects of interacting with others online is a critical aspect of becoming active learners and successful e-moderators.

Emotions

There are several ways of expressing your feelings online. Whatever method you choose, remember that the recipient may not look at it for days, by which time your feelings may have modified.

E-tivity 2.7

Purpose: to practise expressing emotion.

Task: reply with feeling in *E-tivity 2. 7* to. . .

'I've just heard that I've received a major research grant for exploring online learning.'

or to

'Your last reply to me was really rude!'

Respond: (with empathy!) to any message that makes you feel upset or amused.

Here is one participant's summary of responses to this e-tivity. Note that he succeeded in demonstrating good e-moderating skills by ending his message with a challenging question.

The forum about emotional responses was addressed with enthusiasm by all who posted. After everyone had a go at measured and careful responses and expression, the congratulations flowed like honey and would have made anyone on the receiving end extremely chuffed. I was amazed how many ways there are at expressing pleasure and support in writing. Only one or two people admitted that they wished they'd got the grant instead . . . and one tried a little guilt to divert some resources her way! When it comes to saying sorry, there was an overall tendency to take the blame for the perceived rudeness. The exception to this was by one or two of the male forum posters who, whilst apologising for the rudeness, reiterated the gist of their initial message and stood their ground – by far a harder message to write. . . online assertiveness, is it harder to achieve? JH

We continue, at stage 2, with the issue of online time.

How often should I visit?

Successfully learning online or e-moderating depends on a considerable rethink in the use of time. I expect you're finding that out by now! Time is a theme you might like to reflect on throughout this course. One aspect is the frequency of visits or log-ons to your conference.

For a course like this one, a daily visit by the e-convenor seems about right to provide the level of response that participants expect. The e-moderator's behaviour is reflected in the activities of the participant. Do you think a quiet e-moderator will result in quiet participants? On the contrary, participants will simply slope off. Unfortunately, busy e-moderators – replying to every message sent – can bury participants in messages and place themselves centre stage! This, of course, is unfortunate for group and knowledge building between participants.

I recommend looking in most days (say five times a week). I try to fit this in with other occasions when I sit at the PC. I reply immediately to messages that are easy to respond to and make a note of those that aren't and reply later.

If you invite your participants to call in twice a week, they will expect a reply from you when they next visit. To guarantee giving them a response within their timescale, you need to look in more frequently than they do, say three times a week.

If you develop a structured e-tivity, then you will be able to let participants know what they are expected to do and by when, and when you will be back, and for what purpose. Planning in this way is often more comfortable than a free-flow, though maybe less creative?

E-tivity 2.8

Purpose: determine how frequently you should be online and for how long.

Task: reflect on this session, how much time you have spent online and your work pattern of activity, talk to colleagues and learners where you work. You may find some people feel exploited or angry about the time taken working online. Post your thoughts in *E-tivity 2.8*.

Respond: look at those with very different patterns and explore the differences.

Here is a participant's summary of the responses to this e-tivity in one course:

Here is a summary of 'How often should I visit?' Eighteen replies were posted to this forum topic. It was interesting to see a couple of common threads in the replies. First, e-moderators need to recognize that they should facilitate not dominate the online interaction and activity. Second, background activities usually take up a major percentage of the e-moderator's allocated time. J's point regarding the need to educate participants to reasonable expectations and expected turnaround time for queries, postings, and so on seemed very valid to me. The instancy of the Internet creates unreal expectations with some people, and can be a demotivating factor. It was generally agreed that it would be difficult to set a finite number to how often to visit, as it would depend on the age, experience and nature of the forum. LB

At stage 2 we also, fairly gently, introduce the idea of working with diversity and look towards its value in knowledge construction. This simple e-tivity seems to interest many participants and is rich in its responses.

What are our participants' perspectives?

Knowles (1985) (writing before online learning) set out two approaches to teaching and learning:

1.   *Pedagogic* – where learners are treated as if they were children: they know nothing and the teacher decides what they should learn and fills them up with information.

2. *Androgogic* – where the curriculum is negotiated with the learners. Learners bring a good deal of experience to the learning situation – it's much more of a partnership.

Both views can be valid, but an inappropriate one can cause difficulties. Most highly participative adult online learning works better if the e-moderator takes a more androgogic approach. In the online environment a 'schoolish' approach can result in. . . silence, with a smouldering participant somewhere out there.

How do you feel about this general rule: 'Find out what participants know already and build from there?'

E-tivity 2.9

Purpose: to identify ways of helping adults to learn through online interaction.

Task: you are running an online course, which includes working across a number of different countries and cultures. One of your participants e-mails you and says that she is having difficulty in understanding participants from one of the cultural groups. She feels that what they say is irrelevant and often unhelpful. Consider what approach you think might be appropriate to her (pedagogic or androgogic), and post a message you might send to her to *E-tivity 2.9*.

Respond: comment constructively on the messages of others.

Most participants find responding to the problems quite challenging. Some ask for patience and encourage the participants to keep trying to understand. Others put the task of finding the solution back to the complainer.

I think the first thing that I would do is to go to the forum in question and have a look for myself. I don't think I could respond without doing this. If I felt that there was a problem I would plan some sort of activity that might help the participants to achieve common ground: 'Dear Jane, Thanks for your mail and your consistent participation. It is wonderful that we all have the opportunity to work online together like this. It's a really big challenge for people from different cultures to get together in such an environment, what we are doing is really groundbreaking and I'm sure there will be many misunderstandings along the way. I'm glad you want to sort it out for yourself. Do you think some small group work would help?' JH

Via personal e-mail: Alison, in a group like this one where we are working with student from different countries and cultures there will inevitably be occasions where different communication styles – which can be the result of different cultural upbringing – come to face to face. It's important to realize that our own way of dialogue is not the only way of expressing ideas. Many cultures, for example, are less direct than the Anglo–Saxons in expressing themselves. Also, when someone is writing in a language that is not their first language, it is sometimes difficult to determine exactly what they mean. If you are not sure what people mean, or you find what they write unhelpful, then be honest and courteous and gently let them know. Explain how you feel and ask for clarification. I would not suggest highlighting cultural differences (unless they raise the topic first) but just be sensitive and patient. I know this may add time to your workload but hopefully it will be worth it in the end. I'll try to pop into your discussion group and monitor things as well. Let me know if you really find the situation too difficult. We can always swap the groups around but initially I'd really like you to persevere with your group. OK? MC

At this point, participants have reached the end of week two of the course. We ask them to reflect once more, encouraging them to say how they feel as well as how they are thinking! They are also reminded at this point that they should be developing some simple group statements about what they are learning for the 'footprint' area.

This week I've been thinking about the music of time. Since there are no time constraints or set targets, how can the e-moderator judge who is truly passive, and who has just taken a break for a few weeks? And if there are no targets, is there any added value in participation over browsing? MP

And other participants responded:

So true Malcolm, I have begun to realize this myself and will stop 'beating myself up' if my conferences are mainly browsed so long as the history shows readership (i.e. browsing) is very high. Not every conference can or should be highly participatory by all members. GK

Reading the résumés was an enjoyable part of this session. Reading the résumés and the following discussion has made me think that I have underestimated the potential value of résumés to contribute to the online group process and to helping to set the 'tone' for communication. BP

Yes, it is difficult to gauge your response when you can't see the person's body language. Until we work online I don't think that we realize just how difficult. I'm also conscious that I try to think very carefully about my choice of words before I reply as I may upset someone unnecessarily. VR

I have normally learnt in the safety of the classroom environment and all the good things associated with it. Whereas in the past I may have been harsh in the way that I have dealt with non-participating students, I now can empathize with those who may experience difficulties because their learning style is not geared to online learning. In a classroom you can see the expression on a person's face and reflect your behaviour to suit each person; however, online I would really have to ask more question to gauge how students were coping with the hectic and wild world of virtual interaction. JR

Session 3, stage 3: Information exchange

At stage 3 we concentrate on critically important e-moderating skills. We offer a framework based on opening messages, weaving, summarizing and closing, all explored through simple but sequenced e-tivities.

Invitations

Here we explore different ways of inviting participants to take part.

There is no instant recipe, but there are some important ingredients. Be friendly, state the purpose of the discussion clearly, offer some incentive for joining in, make it clear that you want their ideas, and set out something for them to do online and a reason to interact with others. Use great opening messages. Encourage them to send messages so that you can respond encouragingly. Structure, structure, structure; pace, pace, pace!

E-tivity 3.1

Purpose: evaluate messages for 'enticeness'.

Task: evaluate how well the following messages stand up to scrutiny. Reflect on how you could improve on them. Compose one of your own and post it in *E-tivity 3.1*. See how great you can make your opening message!

Respond: by reacting to others' invitations.

Example 1
'Hi, Everyone. Welcome to this conference. Don't be afraid – put some messages up about the course! Moses (I run this conference).'

Example 2
'Hello there. My name's Alison. I'm e-moderating this conference. Please make frequent contributions here. Don't send messages here that should be private. Keep your messages short and try not to offend anyone.

'I'll be putting lots of points related to the topic of this conference here, so be sure to look here each day. Alison'

Clearly, neither message is particularly enticing. Participants are more than ready to critique them and offer suggestions of their own.

> Both of these messages are too authoritarian. Although the second message is friendlier than the first, the style makes it clear who's in charge. Discussion boards should be owned by all those using them, although someone needs to have control. These messages do not give that impression. JD

Instead JD suggests:

> This is your discussion board, so use it frequently and with care. Speak politely, reply with courtesy, debate with intensity, interact with care, and switch the lights out when you leave the building. JD

Here is another response:

> I like Moses' easy style, he's relaxed and welcoming, but he doesn't give
> me much information about the purpose of the conference I'm joining
> – perhaps I'm supposed to know that already? I find Alison's message less
> welcoming since she details all the things I shouldn't do first and it's almost
> a command to contribute. I don't respond well to being told what to do,
> I'm afraid; I need to be told why it's good that I do it. I'm assuming this
> is a general welcome message. I suppose I might have written something
> like this:
>
>> Hi everyone! My name's Lorraine and I'm your tutor for this module.
>> The purpose of this discussion board is to discuss current issues
>> relating to the course and I'll be posting topics here on a regular basis.
>> To ensure you get the most out of this course, please check the board
>> on a regular basis and join in with the conversation. For those of you
>> who have not participated in online discussions before, there is a
>> document on Netiquette to help guide you through the art of
>> e-communication. The first topic for discussion is posted in the next
>> thread. I look forward to hearing from you all.
>
> Lorraine LM

It is at this point in the course (halfway through) that we first introduce the idea
of using resources outside the e-tivity interchanges themselves. This is deliberate.
We wish to show that the key resources are the information knowledge and skills
of the participants themselves. Even when we do introduce use of the Web, we
place it in the context of evaluating, sharing and the relevance and usefulness
of information for active and interactive engagement.

Key sources of information

Electronic information can provide useful stimulus, triggers or 'sparks' for conferences
and e-tivities. Electronic resources stop interaction if overused.
  When using electronic resources we suggest you:

- Indicate why a participant might want to access, read or use them – the benefit
  to them.

- Indicate your view of the quality and validity of the information, for example by commenting on the date, authority of the source, usefulness to you or other ways of evaluating.
- Work out how you can use the resource to encourage participation.

E-tivity 3.6

Purpose: compile a list of useful sources of information for e-moderators.

Task: our aim is to build a list of our favourite sources of information on the Internet for e-moderators. Aim to find *one* source and post the URL in a message, indicating your responses to 1, 2 and 3 above in *E-tivity 3.6.*

Respond: pick out at least one source from another participant and comment on your view of it. Suggest how it might be used as a 'spark' for contribution or to promote interaction.

This e-tivity generally evokes considerable interest and exchange of URLs. One especially interesting outcome is that people from similar disciplines or levels of education tend to 'find' each other online and share ideas.

The penny has dropped! I've been overloading my students with 'content' and then talking to myself! And I thought that fabulous web site added such value! Softly, softly I go now. . . ZP

Barry has introduced me to some great new stuff in the physics area. What he uses for 16- to 18-year-olds will be of great value in my e-tivities for first-year undergraduates. Thanks! AT

At this point, we're heading towards the end of stage 3. We know that there is a fairly steep jump to get participants fully involved in knowledge construction at stage 4. We therefore start to explore the nature of knowledge construction, through a simple e-tivity.

Exchanging information

Many of us are happy to exchange information with others, provided the traffic is not always one-way. The importance of reciprocity for e-moderators is that we should ask questions in order to keep discussions going, and to challenge thinking.

The e-moderator may be the one person who is online every day and has the opportunity to answer all questions first. We should not hurry to provide answers (even if we know them) because this may inhibit participants who have a contribution to make. A common reason given by participants for not posting is that someone has already said what they wanted to say.

E-tivity 3.7

Purpose: being encouraging about the process of exchanging information without being the source of information.

Task: what would you do and why if you saw the following message in your conference: 'I'm trying to find out whether the term moderator means the same in every learning culture.'? Post your reply into *E-tivity 3.7.*

Respond: to other contributions, aiming to get more information by asking a question or adding some other point and inviting comments.

At the end of stage 3 we once again ask for reflections and a reminder of the group 'footprint' responsibility.

Everything seems to have come together this week. It has a very full schedule of activities and, with the need to complete the online group discussion, makes for a very busy time. The e-tivities require a pulling together of a lot of the ideas and info from the rest of the conference, summarising, and making high level plans. They are evaluative at a high level. TK

Content is king? No! Long live e-tivities! BB

Session 4, stage 4: Knowledge construction

At stage 4, we offer two main kinds of e-tivities: designing e-tivities and practising knowledge management skills. The e-tivity sequence at this stage includes a guide to online discussion, opening a topic, seeking information, building knowledge and closing down a topic. As well as introducing knowledge exchange, session 4 offers participants further practice in the skills introduced at stage 3.

Designing e-tivities

These are the keys to structuring and pacing online activity. They provide focus for a group that you may be e-moderating.

Managing the discussion. We offer a four-step discussion guide to help you progress quickly online.

Discussion skills. To help the discussion along you will practise important 'discussion' skills. Instead of providing e-tivities on this subject, we have included a brief resource that you can find in *S4 Resources*.

Designing e-tivities. You have experienced over 15 e-tivities during the course so far. We think they are a good way of engaging participants at each of the five steps, and providing some purpose, structure and pacing to the online learning experience. What do you think? Now is your opportunity to get some practice in their design.

Designing anything is a creative task, and might take a little more time than you think.

Here is a way to begin:

- Start with the end in mind.
- First thing first.
- Think win win.
- Sharpen the saw.
- Be proactive.
- Seek to understand.
- E-moderate.

(After Covey, 1999)

E-tivity 4.1 (allow up to an hour for this one)

Purpose: to practise creating an e-tivity.

Task: bearing the above suggestions in mind, create an e-tivity for a topic of your choice. Here are some side headings for you to work with. If you would like private feedback as well as feedback from your fellow participants, then send a copy to the *E-Convenor.*

- Name of e-tivity?
- Purpose of the e-tivity?
- Stage (of the five stages) it is aimed at?
- How many participants?
- Conference structure?
- E-lapsed time needed?
- E-moderators time?
- E-moderator actions?
- Participant time needed?
- Participant actions?
- Creating interaction?
- How evaluated?

Scroll through the contributions of others – they'll give you further ideas to try.

Responses to this e-tivity are wide and varied. E-convenors give individual feedback and help participants develop their e-tivities to the point that they can try them in their own courses and contexts. In addition, many participants choose to post their e-tivities ideas in the conference and receive contributions from others. Course members also use the posted e-tivities as 'sparks' for their own work. Some of their ideas appear in Resources for Practitioners 5.

In addition to e-tivity building at stage 4, we also offer participants the experience of knowledge construction around a simple topic. The topic itself varies according to the nature of the participants on the course. We have found that in global courses something of rich but generic interest – even one word such as 'Titanic' – will run and run. Or it can be a relevant topic for staff developers in a particular university or discipline – for example, the word 'networking' is successful. It never fails to amaze us that such simple e-tivities result in such rich exchanges.

The spark word or phrase needs to be chosen carefully to be stretching and of interest to the group as well as one that has a range of media and/or approaches associated with it. Resources for Practitioners 5 offer more ideas.

By way of illustration, I show below the sequence of e-tivities around the topic *Dead Poets Society*, a movie about teaching, which also has a number of Web sites available on the Internet.

Giving and seeking information

This information exchange is along the lines of the previous session *but* with a much clearer purpose. This stage enables all participants to attain a similar level of key information about the topic so that all can participate. Aim to share the key points first, about *what you know now*. If details are needed or it is important to share additional background, tell participants about references you know of (eg Web sites) and where to find more information if they want to.

E-tivity 4.3

Purpose: to get everyone up to the same level of information.

Task: brainstorm *what you know now* about the topic *Dead Poets Society.*

Respond: think about the nature of online brainstorming.

Building knowledge

Here we help each of the participants to build knowledge by asking questions, relating the information to other things that they know, and by searching for new information from the Internet. By the end of this e-tivity all will have learnt something – if not about the topic, then about other participants and their reactions to the topic!

E-tivity 4.4

Purpose: to build some new knowledge.

Task: ask searching questions about what you have seen in your *group conference* on *Dead Poets Society.* Challenge a piece of information or ask how it might relate to something else you know about. Post these questions to the *group conference.* Here is a reminder of the e-moderator knowledge construction role, for those adopting this role for the group.

- The contributor needs to be acknowledged in order to be heard. The e-moderator avoids the temptation to discount the experience in any way or to counter it and enter into argument.
- The contribution is available for others to read and so becomes a form of inventory. The e-moderator promotes creation of the inventory in such a way that it can used by others.
- The e-moderator may comment on the sufficiency of the information and views being presented and on the quality of argument surrounding them (if no other participant does this).

These ways ensure that the experiences, whilst valued, are not necessarily considered complete in themselves. The e-moderator models ways of exploring and developing arguments.

Respond: to messages with other questions or by answering questions or by adding ideas or information. . .

We remind participants about the importance of weaving, archiving, summarizing and closure from e-tivities at stage 3.

When you are satisfied that the discussion has run its course, don't leave it in an unfinished state. This would be rather like ending a conversation by walking off without saying goodbye. Be positive and close the discussion with a flourish!

E-tivity 4.5

Purpose: to conclude the discussion on *Dead Poets Society*.

Task: pick up any of the last points in your group conference, summarize them, relate the outcome of the discussions to the purpose of the topic, and thank everyone who took part.

Respond: to the concluding messages of your colleagues.

Not everyone likes this series of e-tivities. Some participants dislike the direct instructions to contribute whilst simultaneously praising the range of responses! Some participants suggest that the clause 'or choose another movie that has inspired you' could be added. However, as you will see, it invokes a huge range of responses.

Dead Poets *summaries*

The singular issue that I learnt from these exercises is that nearly everybody associated 'DPS' with the film. Very few thought outside the square, which leads me to two conclusions: the power of film and media to focus people to a singular line of thought, and the power of search engines and people's willingness to opt for the first solution – overlooking other options. RA

What I gained was the need to be more selective on how I phrase and direct e-tivities in gaining broader views of a topic – promoting wider discussion. RB

I have learnt about the movie. I have learnt how info about the movie can be presented in different ways, and I have learnt something about other people on the course! CC

From Rebecca, I learnt that there is a connection between DPS and the school my son used to attend! From Rose I learnt that this is one of her favourite movies and she has referred to it in lectures she has given on teaching methodology. I re-learnt too what I had forgotten. DPS portrayed a teacher who was passionate about his subject area, believed in each and every one of his students' ability to learn, encouraged creativeness and individual thinking and roused the excitement through his uniqueness in teaching style, and that it dealt with students around ages 11 or 12. MC

Well, the discussion re-activated my interest in the movie and I might even get it out again and re-watch it. Then again I may not! I particularly enjoyed the different ways people approached the activity and so the knowledge being built covered factual information (for those who need to know such stuff) to the more profound. RG

OK, so I've read the initial discussions checked out the questions and read the summaries (thanks guys). Yes, I learnt more about the film and the Society. But more importantly I've learnt (re-learnt?) that people need to be engaged if they are to choose to contribute (unless it's a 'have to' for assessment purposes). The '"what's in it for me" for learners' that Lisa talks about is so critical:

- Being too prescriptive isn't necessarily the best way to engage learners.
- Being too 'loose' also isn't necessarily the best way to engage learners.
- Everyone has something to contribute to add to the whole body of knowledge.
- Reading the question and re-reading and re-reading it again still doesn't mean I'll see all the meaning in it!

(Thanks C. for opening our eyes!). PO

I've learnt that we need to comment carefully on useful or less useful ways of contributing and building on knowledge. All these were included: facts, feelings, links, memories, anecdotes, meanings or extrapolations for teaching practice from the film or the Society. All these were ways we contributed to the whole body of knowledge of the group. I'm not sure that any one way is more or less useful than another. It depends on what is wanted and why it is being gathered. Maybe I'm off the beaten track here but I think that forums can be used to gather knowledge and to explore its meaning, reflect on what has been learnt and then re-form that knowledge into something that (hopefully) is of use to the people who are sharing that experience. Very deep. Hmm. Cheers FF

As always, we provide a 'point of learning' reminder about both personal reflections and group 'footprints'.

We ask for reflections again at the end of stage 4. By now, participants are finding this part of their rhythm of learning and close to 100 per cent of participants post.

> Well, considering I had only limited recollections of the movie *Dead Poets*, I have learnt a lot from the discussions on this topic. For example: who was in it, when it was made, the story behind it and the ways in which it has had an impact on people. Is this knowledge? MC

Other participants responded:

> I guess the question for me would be 'So what?' Can you use this knowledge, Martin? SQ
>
> Well, what I enjoyed was looking at the different ways in which the group approached the challenge of getting 'everyone up to the same level' of knowledge. As Rosanne has so eloquently articulated in her posting, communicating is a rather complex process. The sort of 'forced learning' that I undertook in this e-tivity shows to me how even things that we may not necessarily have any interest in can still communicate new knowledge and demonstrate new ways of thinking. PT
>
> My comment on useful/less useful ways of contributing and building on knowledge is an extension of this. . . I think that there needs to be a 'what's in it for me?' for learners, or they may not feel motivated to complete an activity or participate in a discussion. I also feel that forums work best when they challenge and stimulate people to share their feelings, thoughts and ideas – rather than issue instructions to 'go and find out XYZ then come back and post the answers'. This seems to be a bit too close to the regurgitative style of teaching/learning all too common in classrooms. Now when I use this series of e-tivities in my classes, I'll ask them what they feel as well as what they thought (I think!). DJ
>
> The debate on knowledge construction was interesting. We might have gone even further than the stage 4 of the step model? We raised so many issues about cultural differences, I found really thought-provoking because

I haven't a clue about the best way to approach it in some circumstances. Of course, one doesn't know, often, people's racial or cultural characteristics in this medium and sometimes one does not know their gender either. So the medium can often be used *as if* in a culture-, race- and gender-free environment. Which of course it's NOT! So when I was confronted with an issue like this, it brought me back to reality with a jolt! MD

My reflection. I've held up a mirror on my prejudices. They weren't all that pretty. I looked at my knowledge. It was bigger than I thought. I looked at my confidence compared to when I start only four weeks ago. . . it was a tiny speck then. . . it now nearly, but not quite fills the frame of my looking glass. Who would have thought knowledge was so shiny? KS

These e-tivities are unrelenting masters – I hear them calling me from afar. . . how do you do this, Gilly? And yet I love my fellow participants to death. Oh sorry, maybe I shouldn't say that! Now to get my hands on some e-tivities for myself, for the course that I teach. . . AS

This is real, this is! My brain is expanding, sucking up stuff through my keyboard. PS

Session 5, stage 5: Development

Stage 5 explores the issues around both personal development and enabling the development of others.

The e-moderator role in development

As e-moderator, you can take your cue from the ways the participants behave online. In this, the fifth stage, participants should be comfortable with the medium, be sociable and socialized, be able to exchange information, take part in e-tivities and build knowledge with others. They should also begin to feel they could help others and integrate others arriving at stages 1 and 2. You will know that you are doing well as an e-moderator if productive online activity takes place.

Participants develop at different rates and their needs vary. The challenge is to be helpful as participants continue to develop but without interference or control from the e-moderator: a delicate balance.

At this stage, ask yourself, 'How can I encourage the participants to clarify, articulate and achieve their development needs?'

E-tivity 5.1

Purpose: to identify development needs.

Task: what do you think the underlying needs are from this message? Post your thoughts in *E-tivity 5.1.*'I wish the e-moderator of this online course had given us clear ground rules for how we should communicate with each other. It would have saved me such a lot of time, particularly at such a busy time of the year.'

Respond: to the views of others to expand your own.

At this stage in the course we encourage personal development and a short, structured action plan.

Building a development plan

You may have a favourite format for your development plans, but if not, the outline example below may help. Many plans will contain five steps like this one.

Personal development plan example

- *Development needs:* to achieve greater participation in online working.
- *Development objective:* to increase participation from three messages per week per participant to five messages a week within a five-week course. (A SMART objective again!)
- *Strategy:* to be more encouraging to participants.
- *Actions:*
  - respond within 24 hours to all messages that look as if a response is required;
  - contact participants directly if they have not made a contribution for three days;
  - provide an incentive for each participant to make a contribution.
- *Evaluation:* count the number of messages per participant per week.

E-tivity 5.2

Purpose: to plan for personal development in e-moderating skills.

Task: draw up your own development plan focusing particularly on the development need that, if met, will make the greatest difference to your e-moderating skills. Send a copy to the *e-convenor* for private feedback and, if you would like feedback from your fellow participants, post it to *E-tivity 5.2.*

Respond: to those participants seeking feedback about their plans.

The entire course and all its conferences

Your course is now a large resource containing your contributions and those of others including the e-convenor. Here is an opportunity to scan through and focus on one of the features of this course.

E-tivity 5.3

Purpose: to focus on the skills of e-moderation.

Task: look through all the messages throughout the entire course. Focus on *one* of:

- the way the conference has been managed;
- how easy it is to read messages from the e-convenor;
- the content of messages.

Identify one contribution that has been particularly helpful to you. Share this contribution and why you have chosen it in *E-tivity 5.3.*

Respond: to the selections of others.

This e-tivity seems very productive as a review and reminder, so long as there are plenty of rich resources for participants to mine.

Here are examples I found between the conferences:

1. Helping to decide purpose:
   - in session 2, Mary told us she tried asynchronous chat and found two sympathetic persons, who encouraged her to keep on going;
   - Val told Mary that there are lots of interesting ideas and comments being exchanged in the conference and where to find things to which she can contribute.
2. Giving feedback and coaching:
   - Evan sent us some reflection questions from T S Eliot (*The Rock's* chorus) on 2 August to think about;
   - Caroline gave feedback on 3 August, thanking Evan and telling him that it expresses her thoughts, beautifully;
   - I also found some coaching or counselling when Caroline told us she guessed 'a happy life depends on balance. Balance between study and pleasure, between analysis and intuition and between work and family.'
3. Responding to questions:
   - Josef asked questions about the exercise with Post-its in section 2.1 on 9 July;
   - e-convenor answered promptly, clarifying what needed to be done on 10 July.
4. Procedures: Gilly Salmon reminded us, on 12 July, section 1, that the title of messages should be accurate.

We also ask for further self-evaluation, based on the course.

While you are waiting for some feedback from me on your development, Ian, try to think about what you have learnt from the *process* of taking part in this course. The course is a rich source of material to use for your development. You don't need to rely on memory – the evidence of what you have achieved is here. There is a complete record of every contribution during the past five weeks still available for your inspection.

What a thought! Now for the challenge! E-convenor

E-tivity 5.4

Purpose: to plan for further development in your e-moderating skills.

Task: take a look at your expectations and objectives in session 1. Consider whether they have been met or not, and give reasons. Would you change them if starting again? Then reflect upon all your contributions posted to all the reflections conferences on this course.

Read through your own contributions and through the other contributions that appeal to you. Explain how you could develop your contribution style significantly.

Now we invite you to add another development objective to your development plan, based upon your further reflections. Post it in *E-tivity 5.4*.

OK! I get it! We've been five staged, haven't we? Somehow I magically want to be a better e-moderator. Now I need to look and consider how to do this. PP

At this point we provide closing e-tivities. These include a final 'footprint' and a relaxed 'cyberbar' area for saying goodbye and making arrangements to stay in touch. We also provide an overview exit questionnaire, which assists in continuous improvement of the course.

Finally – I wouldn't have believed a virtual course could be so 'touchy-feely'! Hugs all round from me too! Thank you all for your postings and comments. GR

I have enjoyed greatly, working with the group on this course. I am continually amazed at how much I feel part of this group – same feelings, discussions and challenges as face to face but with a computer screen! NS

There is still some unfinished business! Other students have brought very considerable expertise in different areas to bear on this programme – in many ways, that has been one of the most memorable features of the five weeks. I have been forced to challenge my pre-conceptions about how I view the medium presently. . . and in the past. MD

One thing that has surprised me is the sadness I feel that the course is ending. I really feel that I've built up good online working relationships and this also has only just started to be true. Possibly I'm a slow learner in this respect (older generation? lack of experience/confidence in being an online worker?). Certainly now I've done this course I can see a lot more possibilities for myself in chatting online and have experimented more with this on the Web just to try it out. Also, it seems a pity that such relationships will be broken and I've offered to set up an MSN 'community' so we can continue with the discussion after the course has ended. I guess that means that we've reached stage 5 and are now independent learners! Good to have got there! TK

Reflections have already been put to good use persuading my senior management to put enough resources into our own online initiatives. In fact the whole course has been good for that, especially the need to be reflective each week, as I've found that many useful ideas have crystallized from that for my own work. VL

I have enjoyed this course immensely and found it a very salutary experience. I find the model powerful, helpful and empowering. I note the issues on time management and shall ponder on the idea of burnout. I did not pace myself terribly well, wanted to go everywhere and read everything (can't bear to miss out) and found that rest of my life was in fair disarray by week 4! HS

We find that it's important to leave the course on screen for a few weeks without e-moderation. Participants often want to browse a little or pick up URLs or e-mail addresses from messages. However, activity ceases within three weeks.

Evaluation

I've looked so far at the five stages in detail. Now I turn to the matter of overall course evaluation. Here are two examples from courses that have been run, a university staff development course and a global course.

Stories from the e-tivities front line: story 3

University of Glamorgan e-college project: online staff development in blackboard

The core activity of the University of Glamorgan (http://www.glam.ac.uk) is traditional delivery of courses at the university campus and through agreements with its associate and other partner colleges. Most lecturing staff have experience only in face-to-face methods of teaching. A few have been involved with traditional print-based distance learning. It was decided to build on this experience and success and to work with partners in the public, private and voluntary sectors to widen the accessibility of the university's business and management courses through new methods of delivery, piloted through the enterprise college (e-college) initiative (http://www.enterprise collegewales.co.uk).

The concept of the project is based upon forming an alliance of complementary organizations in the commercial, educational, media, and communications, public and voluntary sector to deliver training and skills development. The e-college initiative provides the additional flexibility of training and support of the university's students through online entrepreneurial programmes. The flexibility of online delivery removes barriers and reaches an increased constituency of individuals, businesses (particularly those in the small and medium enterprise sector), and public- and voluntary-sector bodies. European structural funds support the development of course material and the delivery of the training for staff. Students are able to study at home, at work and at the college campus and they have access to leased computer equipment, installed in their homes. The e-college initiative provides a significant opportunity for the university to evaluate the development, delivery and assessment of e-learning and to create a pedagogy or androgogy for this form of education.

In order to provide staff with some expertise in e-moderating, the e-college undertook a major staff development programme. Unusually, staff development was put in place prior to going live with students, and staff appreciated this development. The programme was based on an online asynchronous participative programme in Blackboard. It used the five-stage model of e-moderating development as a framework and interactive activities (e-tivities) to maintain interest and interaction between participants. The staff development programme was built and run on the e-college's server. Staff were expected to take part around three hours per week over a five week period in September and October 2001. Overall aims of the training programme were:

- to provide lecturers with the skills to access and use Blackboard conferencing and to undertake a range of tasks online;
- to provide lecturers with the experience and confidence to use the online discussion system as a key resource in building a student based online learning community, and enabling mobilization of the learning of those students through simple interactive and e-moderated participation (called e-tivities);
- enable lecturers to become active members of an online community for e-college e-moderators participating in and contributing to the college's successes, achievement and online interaction.

Evaluation

The online programme introduced a set of simple motivational goals, by requiring participants to reflect 'deliberately' on learning at each stage. They were encouraged to take part, to post at least one message at each of the five stages, to contribute to the 'reflections' conferences, to complete their exit questionnaires – and only then to ask for their certificate of completion.

Results

Thirty-four lecturers involved in the e-college project started the course on or around 10 September 2001. Twenty-seven successfully completed the course by mid-October 2001. Another seven continued to work through the online activities more slowly.

Although staff found the online e-moderation development programme very challenging, nearly all appreciated the opportunity to take part, and felt that they had achieved the objectives. Some of their final reflections are copied below:

> It also made me realize that e-moderating is not something you can do in small parcels of time (the odd hour between classes). It needs more attention and thought than that. ES (December 2001)
>
> I can't believe I've actually reached this stage – final reflections. Overall, I have found the course beneficial. I feel that my confidence of online learning has increased and my navigation skills have certainly improved (although they still are far from perfect). I also feel that I have a better understanding and know-ledge of e-learning. This course has, however, also made me realize just how much more I've got to learn – I think there is a very steep learning curve ahead of me. GG (October 2001)
>
> I have enjoyed the course and I feel I have learned a lot. I now feel more confident about my navigation skills and a little more confident about my e-moderating skills. I will be even more confident once I have tried it for real. Unlike some, I enjoyed the early stages. Finding out so much about each other helped me feel even more the importance of online socialization. NJ (October 2001)

Dr Norah Jones, the Project Manager, wrote:

> The programme was a success at two levels. First, it enabled us to gain greater confidence in using the software package (Blackboard), and secondly, we were able to appreciate the need to fully engage e-learners. We also benefited by staff from many different locations in Wales working together online and getting to know each other through the development programme. We see this form of staff development as essential and plan to spread development of this kind across the University for other e-learning projects. (December 2001)

Stories from the e-tivities front line: story 4 — the global e-tivities course

The drivers for the course

Following the publication of my book *E-moderating* in May 2000, many educators asked me how they could experience online teaching and learning for themselves, start to develop their skills and explore the ideas in the book. These requests came from all over the world. People also wished to have the opportunity to work with others from their own disciplines but, in other countries, university lecturers wanted to understand more about e-learning approaches in corporate training; schoolteachers wanted to get involved, too. A critical issue is that very few teachers, at any level of education, have taken part in online courses for their own professional and personal development. Late in 2000, Centrinity Inc (http://www.centrinity.com), a Canadian-based company, agreed to work with me to provide a fully online course to meet this audience and requirements.

The course was developed in FirstClass software and hosted by Embanet. The first course went live on 1 March 2001 and monthly starts are now offered. Each course attracts between 6 and 25 participants and each is a mix of university lecturers, corporate developers, college lecturers and schoolteachers. The course has attracted participants from every continent in the world. Even in our cynical global society, this brings interest and excitement to the participants. As one, a participant in the third e-moderating course said, referring to its global reach: 'So! This is what online learning looks like from space!'

The five-stage model was used to provide an overall framework and scaffold for the course, and the course was based entirely on e-tivities. We plan for a wide range of prior knowledge and/or experience of online learning and training among the participants. Each has his or her own 'map' of the topic and differing needs. The online course also helps participants to explore their attitudes to online learning and its meaning for their own teaching.

In December 2000 I undertook an evaluation of the global course based on the first 100 completions (Salmon, 2001). At that time we had seen 30 participants located in the UK and 12 from the continent of Europe, 27 from Australia, 16 from South America, eight from the United States and Canada, and seven from Asia. Thirty-four of them were working at universities and 28 in vocational training. Nineteen came from professional networks, 13 from corporate training and 6 from school teaching. Seventy-eight per cent had English as a first language, the rest spoke a variety of other European languages as their mother tongue. Seventy-two per cent of these fully completed the course and received their Certificate of Participation.

Outcomes of the evaluation

- I analysed their 'point of learning' reflections at each of the five stages, using cognitive mapping (Salmon, 2000a), and their exit questionnaires, using quantitative techniques. I contacted all dropouts individually.

- I used the evaluation as an action research tool and developed the second version of the course, which is described. I made changes to the structure of the e-tivities by explicitly adding the requirement to respond to others' messages. I also added small group work from the beginning of the course process, and the 'footprint' requirement.
- Those dropping out typically had technical problems, most of which were solved later so that they were able to start the course on another date.
- Overall, we found that participants were extremely interested in and supportive both of each other and of each other's teaching and learning environments and values. Individuals from different disciplines, levels of education were able to share ideas on e-tivities successfully.
- E-convenors had kept a record of exactly how much time they needed to spend on ensuring the success of the course. We discovered that the 25 hours over five weeks required from around each of around 15 participants, needed around 30 hours from the e-convenors to make it a success. Much of their time and energy was spent at stage 1 in welcoming and getting participants comfortable and started and in responding to individual e-tivities and development plans at stage 5.

I know that reading about the five-stage model and about e-tivities is not as exciting as trying them out for yourself. Chapter 4 goes on to describe how to go about creating your very own magical e-tivities, which are right for your topic and your participants.

For extra magic, try Resources for Practitioners 8 and 10. Resources for Practitioners 6 gives examples showing how a series of e-tivities can be combined into programmes.

Chapter 4

Creating e-tivities

This chapter will help you to develop techniques for creating high-quality e-tivities for use within your course, programme, community or in any other context. It explores how to establish enjoyable and successful e-tivities using asynchronous text-based conferencing and the Internet as a vehicle. All of the Resources for Practitioners in Part II should give you further ideas and inspiration.

The whole e-tivity process should be geared towards engaging participants in active online learning that results in their achieving the outcomes that they and you desire. Therein lies the benefit for the participants and the purpose of all the pedagogical activity. This seems obvious, yet I know it is easy to become focused on providing wonderful resources or to become excited about the potential of the technology and then to wonder why people do not want to take part, or, if they do, why they experience difficulties.

That's why I call the e-tivity instructional message the 'invitation' – this word helps to remind me that I'm looking for a response from others and I'm planning some social (learning) event.

As an ideal, aim for participants to contribute positively, actively, constructively and interactively. I know this is easier said than done. However, I hope you will use the principles in this chapter and try out some e-tivities that seem meaningful to you. A great advantage is that they can be easily changed for a second try, or scaled up for increased numbers or to highlight them if they are successful. Give attention to active engagement, participation, the emotional aspects of learning and new constructs of time and I know that the outcomes will surpass your best expectations!

E-tivities require careful construction. Most of the groundwork should be prepared in advance of the participants' arrival. Finding, structuring and delivering online 'content' is less important than teaching techniques when designing and running e-tivities. With good design and preparation, the e-moderators role in running the e-tivities becomes easier. So let's get started!

The e-tivity process

First I explain some general principles and then I explore them further with examples.

Building e-tivities: key principles

- Decide in advance of the participants logging on what you expect them to do and what the e-moderators will do.
- Ensure that the participants are clear about your intended objectives for an e-tivity. Start with the end in mind.
- Ensure that your planned evaluation or assessment meets the purpose(s) of the e-tivity. If assessment is involved, look for alignment with *tasks*. Attempts to forcefully create participation through direct assessment are rarely successful.
- Build in motivation as part of the process of undertaking the e-tivity itself and not as something separate from it. Motivation occurs because of the learning activities. Avoid trying to motivate people simply to log on and 'discuss'. Instead, provide an e-tivity that makes taking part worthwhile.
- Create an experience that is complete and worthwhile in itself. This includes setting short-term goals but ensuring that there is a satisfying process and 'flow' of actions. In practice, e-moderators need to exercise judgement about when to go with the flow and when to guide participants towards expected outcomes.
- Be highly sensitive to timing and pacing. Divide the e-tivity up into bite-sized chunks of no more than two or three weeks' work for a complete e-tivity – less if possible.
- If you offer more than one e-tivity at a time, build them together in a coherent way to create a 'programme'. Use the five-stage model.
- Ensure that the e-tivities are in some way focused on sharing, shaping, elaborating or deepening understanding.
- Ensure that participants need to work together in some way to achieve the learning outcomes. If you cannot see the way to make working together worthwhile, maybe using e-tivities is not the best approach?
- Be generous in allocating e-moderator time, especially if the e-tivity is geared towards stages 1–3.

- Be ready, be prepared, and don't be surprised at serendipitous events.
- Aim to provide just one invitational message, which contains everything needed to take part. *Each invitational message e-tivity should include*:
  - The purpose of the e-tivity (why the participants are doing it). If the e-tivities are assessed, indicate what might indicate success and how participants can achieve it.
  - What participants should do and how they can go about doing it.
  - How long it should or could take. An idea of when the e-tivity starts and when it should finish.
  - How the participants should work together.

Resources for Practitioners 1 and 2 offer some 'get started' design checklists.

E-tivity purpose

I think of objectives as the stated anticipated result or outcomes of an e-tivity – what I expect it to deliver. Learning outcomes mean to me what the participants can expect to get out of the experience for themselves. For e-tivities, in the spirit of constructivism, I prefer to group these objectives together and call them 'purpose'. In other words, purpose implies a somewhat broader framework or intention. Often, online, the outcomes are more variable than originally intended! However, make sure that you can, if necessary, provide a rationale for the e-tivity in terms of outcomes for those participants who ask.

You will find that participants often want to discuss the purpose of an e-tivity between themselves. This is often a productive discussion and will stimulate people to take part. The shared purpose promotes the e-tivity itself and gives it meaning. However, sometimes e-moderators will need to encourage people to 'go with the flow' and reflect later. Individual participants may have their own agendas in addition to a shared purpose.

At stages 1, 2 and 3 you might need to state the purpose at the beginning of the e-tivity. At stages 4 and 5, purposes can be negotiated. This is how participants start to gain ownership of the learning. However, most importantly, shared understanding is needed of the *task* with which the participants are engaged. This is why careful pacing and consistent instructions are critical.

E-tivity and assessment

Biggs (1999b) offers us the idea of 'alignment' in teaching and assessment. Overtly separate assessment activities break the flow of the e-tivity processes. Your assessment strategies are likely to be more successful, discriminatory and fair if they arise 'naturally' out of the e-tivities. There are two main ways of coming closer to compatibility between e-tivities and assessment. One is by using electronic means through the technology platform itself, and the other is using reflective and collaborative outcomes to align assessment with the teaching and learning characteristics of e-tivities. Both have their own advantages and challenges.

You might be interested in the Open University's approach to e-assignments. Tutor-marked assignments are a critically important part of the OU's assessment, teaching and feedback methods. Since 1995 the OU has deployed an 'in-house' system of electronic assignment, submission marking, tracking and grade recording. The e-system involves a student creating his or her assignment electronically, posting the 'zipped up' assignment to a holding Web site that also records its receipt and identifies and notifies the student's tutor. The tutor then 'collects' and downloads it from the site, and marks it on screen using a software tool or features in Word such as 'comments'. The tutor then returns the marked assignment back to the Web site, zipped up. The assignment score is automatically transferred to the university's recording system. Copies of some assignments are extracted for monitoring, a part of the quality-assurance processes. The student collects the marked script. Currently around 10 per cent of assignments are submitted electronically – a total of around 100,000 assignments each year (Walker, 2002). The rest still use a post and paper system.

The challenges presented by the e-system are that tutors need training to assess and mark electronically, just as they need training to e-moderate. There are many concerns about the system 'going down' (although post, even in the UK, was never completely reliable). It is important for everyone involved to be using compatible software. However, the system is fast and there is secure recording and traceability of the marks and the processes. The turnaround times from student to tutor and back again are much faster than by paper and post. Once tutors get used to the system, they can mark and provide teaching feedback more creatively and effectively.

Alignment with online teaching and learning processes and approaches is a little harder to achieve. When developing e-tivities, we need to look right from the start at how the learning can be appropriately assessed, whether based on individual or group work. E-tivities rarely produce the 'right' answer, and therefore assessment and outcomes can be judged in a number of ways. Make this clear to participants. Stage 5 of Resources for Practitioners 5 offers you a range of ideas.

There may be complex power and emotional issues at play, and e-moderators need both to be sensitive and to maintain authority (Trehan and Reynolds, 2001). However, if you succeed in getting groups of participants working productively together at stages 4 and 5, then they are already involved in mutual and supportive feedback and evaluation of each other's work through their ongoing interaction (McConnell, 1999). The scene is thus set for compatible assessment procedures. If the purpose of an e-tivity is carefully worked out, this will often give you a clue as to how it can be assessed. Or, if you're brave, you can encourage groups to design their own assessments. So essentially I'm suggesting that the principles for e-tivities also apply to assessment.

If you are evaluating or assessing then you will need to indicate the level or degree of acceptable performance. Inevitably, what you will look for in assessment is the outcome that you hoped for, and, as you also need to learn for yourself, any outcomes that you didn't plan for. It is a mistake to try to control for every possible eventuality. Furthermore, if you change one thing about an e-tivity for a second try at it – for example, you give a little less or more time to one part or use a different 'spark' – you will find that the whole e-tivity changes and hence the assessment.

The use of electronic resources in assignments may increase opportunities for plagiarism and cheating. You can find out more about the potential and hence how to avoid it (Croucher, 1996). Some e-moderators have told me they are worried that a student may be able to change the grades awarded. The OU system I have described avoids such problems because it records receipt and marks awarded at each stage. I suggest you use a system of careful recording and keep electronic copies, at least for the duration of the course and beyond.

The Internet has led to new methods of cheating for those learners who are inclined to do so. For example, where assessment is based on individual written work, such as essays or dissertations, use of technology may simply make it easier for participants to present work that they have not personally authored. Of course technology can also be used to detect cheating. (Take a look, for example, at www. plagiarism.org.) All universities have policies about plagiarism and cheating that need to be reinforced in the online environment. A useful set of guidelines can be found published by JISC in the UK (Carroll and Appleton, 2001).

It is important to establish and publish what you mean by the difference between collaborating and cheating. Encourage participants to use, but carefully attribute, copied remarks and quotes from messages. There is a fine dividing line between 'compiling' or 'summarizing' and 'plagiarizing'. See Resources for Practitioners 30. Perhaps you could try an e-tivity at stages one or two to address and explore these words directly.

Fear of failure is often cited as a common motivation for cheating (Pitt, 2001). Successfully taking students through a scaffold or contingent approach to learning online offers a sense of involvement and hence potentially less desire to gain an *unfair* advantage over other participants.

E-tivity actions

Be very specific about what you need your participants actually to *do*. I suggest you use verbs as instructions and invitations for the task. At stages 1 to 3, I like the simple online verbs of 'post' and 'respond to' but there are many others. See Resources for Practitioners 4. However, participants' responses may be unpredictable. They may do a variety of things that you don't expect. We consider almost any activity to be acceptable if it is consistent with task or group progress.

There are special aspects of working online that may interfere with active learning and which need to be taken into account in the design of the e-tivity task. The first is the role of emotions. Feelings such as frustration or anger are typically associated with either the technology appearing not to work properly, or are affected by an incident with another participant or the e-moderator. Emotions associated with the technology and the e-moderating are commonest at stages 1 and 2, and relationships with other participants at stages 3 and 4. By stage 5, participants can usually handle both. Developing e-tivities that are appropriate for the stage in the model, whilst encouraging participants to acquire the skills to move up through the scaffold, will help them to acquire skills in handling emotions.

See Resources for Practitioners 5, 10 and 11 for more ideas. The work of Terry Mayes and colleagues on 'turning discussions into learning tasks' is helpful. If you would like a taxonomy of tasks, look at Mayes *et al* (2002: 219).

Build in reflection

There are many ways to reflect. Some writers argue that reflection is essentially an independent activity. Other writers stress the importance of collaboration to the reflection process (Rose, 1992). Schön distinguishes between reflection on action (reflection after practice has been completed) and reflection in action (thinking that takes place in the midst of practice). I suggest you try out both reflection in action and reflection on action in your e-tivities and programmes because both are valuable. For example, in the course I describe in Chapter 3 we offer a weekly 'point of learning' reflection opportunity (reflection in action). However, in addition we offer a variety of opportunities for looking back and evaluating aspects of the dialogue during the last week of the course (reflection on action).

Some e-tivity designers use the idea of encouraging learners first of all to recall a familiar experience as a preparation for introducing them to a new one. The idea here is that experiences need to be interrogated and perhaps tested and challenged to avoid the unconscious assumptions that may reduce creativity and flexibility in attempting to understand or resolve a problem or explore a scenario. Another key aspect of learning through reflective processes is that each adult learner will have different ways of dealing with ideas, using perhaps their well-established learning styles.

Reflection will be easier for some participants than others. Some people enjoy it very much, some prefer to 'push on'. However, as I think reflection is so important, I always include it as an essential activity. One point to emphasize: make it clear you are looking for participants' views, feelings, experiences and ideas. So this is certainly one time when they can start their sentences with 'I'. But encourage them to end their message with a question or challenge to others to encourage those others to reflect too.

As with all the e-tivities, I suggest you indicate why you are inviting participants to reflect. In our courses, I pose a 'point of learning' reflective question at key points and ask participants to look back through the course on a regular basis. They are invited to respond to our questions at the end of each session, usually once a week, and to the postings of others throughout. We also encourage them to revisit their own responses at any time. Almost all active participants express surprise, even amazement, when they glance back at what they have done, as the following examples show.

Seeing other points of view:

> I have tried on three different occasions to respond to this activity, but each time I enter the conference, there is another person's reflections, which makes me reflect in a way not previously thought of. I think all the contributions to this section are interesting and thoughtful – that to respond to one is just not fair! NS

Recording emotions:

> Some interesting reflections posted for this e-tivity and it is heartening to know that others are feeling the same as me – being an e-learner has made me see the other side of the coin. I have learned a lot about learning online – a whole range of emotions from feeling very lonely at times, experiencing happiness when I achieve something and guilt when I know I am not contributing as much as I should be. CH

E-tivity invitations

Few of us are really skilled at writing concise and effective instructions for word-based messages. The skill improves with practice and with feedback. It is particularly easy to create ambiguity in the task invitation. So I suggest that you test out your instructions on naïve users, preferably potential participants (but if these are not available then your colleagues or your children) to see what they make of them.

Try to ensure that all the information that participants need to post their first message in response is contained in one online message – and one screenful if possible. If you 'send' participants out onto the Web, a few may not come back. If you attach a file to a message, download times and hence potential frustrations are increased.

Titles for e-tivities are very important. Think headlines! They should both give information, invite to take part, entice and distinguish one e-tivity from another. As you saw in Chapter 3, we also use numbers to indicate the stage of the model and the sequence of the e-tivities.

Incidentally, most conferencing software takes a title forward when participants reply, so the title you choose will probably appear many times and affect the online action. E-moderators should advise participants on the importance of careful titles, and about changing them in the headers of messages when topics change and develop. Participants expect the messages to contain roughly what they say in the title and may consider it impolite if they do not. It helps to create focus, and makes the e-moderators' jobs of weaving, archiving and summarizing much easier.

It is a good idea to ensure that messages are easily printed. We don't encourage participants to do this since we think that part of their induction needs to involve learning to work with on-screen messages. However, some people will want to print them – and why not?

E-tivity time

The use and experience of time is a major aspect of successful e-tivities. Time takes on a new dimension online. Working asynchronously involves a radical rethink – not only of learning or teaching time but also of other aspects of life. Most people find this very difficult indeed to start with. By providing a clear indication of an expectation of active contribution and by pacing the e-tivity, you will help participants to make the adjustments to their lives. You might like to think about providing regular activities that provide a framework – e-tivities that start and finish at predictable times and actions that occur regularly, such as the e-moderator's summary. In addition, you need to provide interest and motivation through underlying rhythm. Engaging in authentic tasks and working with others can provide this idea of rhythm. Using clear start and finish times by the clock and the calendar enables synchronization and co-ordination of group activities. Such pacing needs to appear in the e-tivities because participants will not meet often 'by chance' online to co-ordinate for themselves.

We frequently feel we do not have enough clock time and most people are very sensitive to unproductive or waste of time. If we focus on such a measurement of time, we can often become very alarmed about 'how much time' online is taking up. However, we all also know that we do not feel or experience time in the linear way a clock suggests. This is known as 'felt' time and it's linked directly to how connected we are to what we are doing. If we feel engaged and connected, then we focus less on time passing and experience time quite differently. If you are successful in building effective e-tivities, you may notice the reduction of the huge anxiety about the use of clock time. (Unfortunately, when participants log off, the software will probably tell them anyway!)

Participants and their e-moderators will experience time in all sorts of ways when working online. One key aspect is the complexity associated with asynchronicity. For example, in the course described in Chapter 3, participants log on from around the globe and the course is always open. Participants take part according to their quite individual work patterns and locations around the world.

Here is a little extract. It's from a novel and the author is describing a relationship that is developing based on exchange of letters, but I think it illustrates the experience of asynchronicity most graphically:

[B]y the time you open a letter of mine and accept its truth, I am already somewhere else. When I read your letters, I am actually inside a moment of yours that has passed; I am with you inside a time you are no longer inhabiting. This works out to each of us being faithful to each other's abandoned moments. . . (Grossman, 2002: 107)

Remember that 'overfilling' an e-tivity is the enemy of active engagement online. If you provide too many resources, your participants will use them and have little time for each other.

When designing e-tivities and providing invitations to take part, you need to take account of the time you expect participants to be online, responding both to your e-tivities invitations and to each other. It will be fairly easy to determine how long they may need to respond individually to your instructions. If necessary you can get learners to test this. However, it's harder to tell how long they'll need to spend responding to each other. As a rough rule of thumb, I'd suggest that what might take a half an hour with a group of 10 face to face might take one week *elapsed* time online, if each participant came back three times, read other people's messages and posted three of his or her own. The elapsed time is just as important as the actual online time because participants may think a little about the e-tivities whilst going about their everyday tasks and engaging in 'reflection'.

It's really easy, when designing e-tivities, to imagine that participants are somehow in a 'bubble' that will enable them to focus on the e-tivity and give it their best attention – in other words, that they have distinctive time to give to their online learning. Of course this is very rarely the case. I've noticed that when I'm working online, both family and colleagues interrupt me in a way they simply would not if I were in a face-to-face meeting or talking on the telephone. University, college or corporate participants may be in a learning resource centre or a library with other distractions, or they may be on a train or at an airport, where real linear time may interrupt their online time at any moment. A few learners (and e-moderators) are good at setting up their desks and their computers in such a way that they signal to the rest of the world, and to the people they live or work with, that they are fully engaged. But such people are rare. You can productively try an e-tivity at stage 1 that encourages sharing of ideas on avoiding distractions! But we need to see online e-tivity time as integrated as possible with everyone's lives and attention. Providing small discrete 'chunks' of tasks helps since these can be satisfying in themselves. Providing software that takes the user back to the place they left is some people's solution.

I have found that e-moderators have a strong tendency to underestimate the amount of time that is needed for achieving any one aspect of an e-tivity. In addition, and conversely, novice e-tivity designers frequently imagine quite long timescales with a multiplicity of complex e-tivities. These are really hard to achieve successfully with asynchronous online groups. An elapsed time of 18 days overall, with paced e-tivities such as one individual response and one group response, is more realistic and successful in creating active engagement.

The most time-consuming aspect of e-moderating is making good summaries. However, summaries save a huge amount of participants' time, and increase learning and feedback. They are a particular boon to latecomers, who may otherwise be daunted by the number of messages awaiting them when they log on. Summaries can also provide an opportunity to encourage participants to contribute: if no one is prepared to offer a full summary, then participants can be encouraged to offer one or two suggestions that the e-moderator can then build up into a summary.

I suggest that you develop e-tivities that address issues of working in online time from stage 1 onwards. At stages 3 and 4, creative e-moderators find ways of relating these to their discipline – such as science or literature.

Participants new to online learning always seem surprised about the use of their time:

I've enjoyed the week and am looking forward to the next. A fear or concern, however, is that of being in a constant state of catch-up. One of the problems I've had is that I log on to read the new messages and then come back later when I've thought of replies. By then everything has moved on. I guess this is driven by a fear of wanting to get 'the right answer' and having to spend time on a considered contribution. But I'm beginning to realize that it's the trying out of ideas that's important and that a supportive group is a good place to do that. MD

I am left uncomfortable at my intermittent presence caused by other commitments during this first week – I expect to be better organized after the next week. However, I have learned already the value of asynchronous discussion. I have been able to follow the conference and its conversations even after extended absence. I may become less reactive in the near future! RC

I have the pleasure of doing this course in work time, but it is easy to get distracted by the everyday tasks. . . [I] log on as often as possible (ideally at least once a day), even if it is only for a short time. SC

I think the hardest thing so far has been finding time, always a tricky issue! Just skimming through messages is quick, but thinking about things and writing for the e-tivities is more time-consuming. I confess to doing the e-tivities but only writing about some not all of them. SH

All in all have enjoyed experience to date and look forward to getting down to some more proper discussion with everyone (am conscious have not 'met' all course members yet and would like to – must get up earlier!). HS

What about e-mod's time? Much more than you think. Needs discipline to say I won't keep logging on just to have another peek at how it's going. . . and then get totally carried away and time gets eaten up. . . Obviously it varies with the group – but academics are a case in point: they generate so many messages! (Says he, from bitter experience!) KG

I've explored designing and e-moderating for aspects of time in Resources for Practitioners 13–19.

Number of participants

Smallish groups work most easily online. This is unsurprising because each individual comes to know other members of the group more easily – each is encouraged to contribute actively and more sustained engagement is thus achieved. We find that groups of 12 to 20 participants work really well. They can be successfully divided into smaller groups and put together again within e-tivity processes.

We usually appoint one trained part-time e-moderator for groups up to 20, with well-structured e-tivities. We have two e-moderators working together for larger groups. With these numbers, e-moderators can be effective and experience work satisfaction, and burnout is avoided.

With larger groups there is a risk that individuals will not participate because they see that others have already made the point they wish to make. The volume of messages tends to put off all but the most active participants, and lurking and vicarious learning are common. However, the way to involve bigger groups and larger number of participants is very regular archiving and summarizing of messages – even daily if necessary. See Resources for Practitioners 30. If you carefully structure your e-tivities, you can start with more participants, but at some point smaller groups will need to relate to each other, especially at stage 4.

On the other hand, there are also risks with small groups. With a group of, say, six, if one or two drop out for any reason, those that are left behind feel bereft and put-upon, and the group may have too few members to be self-sustaining. Stage 1 e-tivities are also often slow to get started because of technical problems, so we generally run them with larger groups and allow a little more time.

One word of warning. You need to be very specific about who is in which group in your e-tivity invitational message. Unlike in face-to-face situations, where participants can quickly and easily sort themselves into groups, it is possible to waste a week just getting into teams online. The easiest way is to specify the maximum size of each group and fill them up on the basis of 'first come, first served'. (We call this method 'leaving buses'.) You might also use criteria such as month of birth or surnames. If you want to form groups based on prior checks or tests then allow extra time. However, as participants reach stage 4 e-tivities they may be better able to organize themselves online.

Resources for Practitioners 9 is about collaborative groups.

Designing for lower costs

Some organizations believe that they can obtain a better return on their investment in e-learning by disposing entirely of lecturer, trainer or e-moderating costs. From the rest of this book, you will see that I think that discarding human intervention is very rarely appropriate or successful. Enormous value is added to the participant experience by skilled e-moderation. However, structured, paced and carefully constructed e-tivities reduce the amount of e-moderator time, and directly affect satisfactory learning outcomes, adding value to the investment. Ash and Bacsich (2002) include the importance of universality and good pedagogy.

E-tivities take time to design properly and require 'space' and experimentation. However, one e-moderator can design an e-tivity that can be used by many groups. It is important to *design* interaction time down and avoid the e-moderator feeling that he or she must respond to every message.

Skilled and trained e-moderators can often handle large numbers of students online, if well-constructed e-tivity programmes are used. Using cheaper people to support participants, such as graduate students or five-stage model alumni, often helps. At stages 1–3 the e-moderator will need to spend a fair amount of time getting the e-tivities going. At stages 4 and 5 he or she can log on less often, but doing good plenary and summaries can be demanding.

There seems to be an overall optimum point on costs at around 30 or 40 participants to one e-moderator (Rumble, 2001). Most well-designed e-tivities run successfully with a ratio of up to 20 participants to one e-moderator, so it's best to have one (well-trained) e-moderator running two groups for optimum cost–benefit.

There is more about costs, and about the choice of technology platforms, in Resources for Practitioners 33 and 34.

Writing invitations

The heart of understanding both writing and taking part in text-based communication is grounded in 'Netspeak'. The way people communicate online is a unique and evolving mix of written and spoken communication. The way we first learn to communicate is through rich face-to-face exchanges, and to most people anything else at first seems 'deficient' or poorer (McAteer *et al*, 2002). In on-screen text messages, people tend to write as if they were talking (Crystal, 2001). Think about the huge variety of talking styles there are! However, written instructions need to be completely clear. They appear to work best if they set up a response and an interchange of information (McAteer *et al*, 2002).

It is important to be brief both in your stimulus and in your invitations – no more than one screenful – and to indicate clearly the kind of brevity you expect in response. This is very challenging if you are to avoid obscurity and ambiguity. Think in terms of the number of sentences in a 'turn' or response, the length of sentences, and the amount of text on the screen.

Online messages, even well-planned ones, can very easily be ambiguous or misinterpreted. An e-moderator does not have quite the same opportunity for spontaneously putting participants right or back on track as a face-to-face facilitator does. It's a really good idea to have your messages checked by one or two naïve users before posting them to a whole group. Also, be prepared, during the e-tivity event itself, for directions to be taken that are unexpected or for e-tivities to be challenged in various ways (this is especially likely to happen from stage 3 onwards). Be prepared to go with the flow. Be prepared for changes the next time the e-tivity is run.

Resources for Practitioners 20 and 21 explore Netspeak a little more.

Sparks

Knowledge involves thinking with information. Participants do not start completely 'cold' but start with some information or knowledge. So, for e-tivities you need to decide what information will be provided as a starting point – the spark to begin the process of group learning and knowledge construction. The e-moderator presents an issue: a dilemma, problem, challenge or model. Use different kinds of data and information, but keep spark paragraphs and links short. If appropriate, you may well wish to provide references, further reading or illustrative links, but try to avoid making any of these necessary for active engagement in the online task.

There are many types of 'sparks' for e-tivities. The main types are providing a small piece of information, a model, concept or example to which participants can react or by asking for views, information or experiences. You might also find a trigger from what participants bring to the e-tivity. Consider what they bring, what might their interests be, what kind of content will interest them, what kind of activities they will want to be engaged in. Here is a stage 1 e-tivity using a well-known learning concept as a spark.

Honey and Mumford wrote about four main individual learning styles. These are:

- *activists* tend to learn best when they are dealing with new problems and experiences;
- *theorists* need to explore the links between ideas and situations;
- *pragmatists*, on the other hand, need to be able to see an obvious link between what they are learning and problems or opportunities with which they are engaged in their work;
- *reflectors* think deeply about the concepts and activities, and tend to give considered responses.

Do you recognize yourself?

Among our participants we are likely to have all preferences and styles. In constructing our course we aim to provide different learning experiences. The e-tivities will provide action for the pragmatists and activists, and reflection for the reflectors and theorists amongst this course.

Resources: *E-moderating*, pp. 72–73 (Salmon, 2000a) and Honey and Mumford (1986).

Purpose: expose your own learning style and find out about the preferred styles of others.

Task: put a short note into the reflections conference about your thoughts at the end of this first session, sharing with others what you have found to be useful, and those things that have been a little harder to do than you expected in this session, indicating how they might be explained by your preferred learning style.

Respond to one message by one other participant that illuminates for you how different learning styles appear in the online world.

Complete this task by the end of week 1 [date]. We will ask you to revisit your answers later on.

Resources for Practitioners 5 shows more examples.

Avoid filling the invitational message with a whole variety of different spark materials, references or links. If you want to provide sparks with more difficulty, depth or breadth, build them into separate e-tivities. Concentrate instead on online actions and state what behaviour is expected of participants during the e-tivity. Be very specific about what you need your participants actually to do. I suggest you use verbs as invitations to the task. I particularly use the active online verbs 'post' and 'respond to', but there are many others. See Resources for Practitioners 4. However, participants' responses may be unpredictable. They may do a variety of things that you don't expect. We consider almost any activity to be acceptable which is consistent with task progress!

The technology

E-tivities are intended to take place online and therefore it's best to aim for online actions and interactions. Participants are allowed to do their thinking and reflection offline, of course! You can ask participants to read a page from a book, or find out information from elsewhere, but the most successful and effective e-tivities do not involve participants frequently going offline to do something else. This is where the characteristics of the technology become important. For me this means that the e-tivity should, if possible, take place fully within the system itself.

Generally the characteristics of text-based asynchronous conferencing mean that everything does not happen at the same time, and is based largely on words. In addition, each individual platform will have special features. For example, the strength of Blackboard is that it allows lecturers to publish materials easily, whereas FirstClass is good for collaborative working. When you design your e-tivities, try to find out about the special characteristics of the software and platform available to you and exploit them to the uttermost! However, once the e-tivities are running and people are taking part, let your knowledge of these characteristics slip into the background. In this way, the technology should enable without demotivating or becoming a focus of attention in itself. After all, we can expect few of the participants to be captivated by the technology and software *per se* rather than as a means to an end.

However, some aspect of the technology platform may prove a barrier. For example, at the moment, in WebCT and Blackboard we have found that we cannot have a neat Web site that includes e-tivity invitational messages and a discussion forum on the same page. You may need to design your e-tivities differently to take account of this, or choose a different platform, or different e-tivities. It really is not necessary to fight battles with the technology about this. I suggest you note carefully what you would like and convey it carefully to the platform providers, explaining clearly why it's important for the e-tivities and the learning outcomes.

Resources for Practitioners 34 focuses on the technologies.

Linking e-tivities to the five-step model

Novices solve problems by following step-by-step procedures, so early e-tivities need to include these. As participants gain competence and expertise, they can handle much more complex ideas. Hence the knowledge useful to novices is different from the knowledge useful to experienced practitioners or learners. In other words, it's our picture of our participants – their needs and competencies and the stage they are at – that determines the tone and focus of the e-tivity. Essentially, you need to be explicit about the development of the groups and the nature of the tasks at each stage. We can thus draw from ideas of gradual group development and the scaffolding provided by the five-stage model.

Here are some general ideas to underpin the process of thinking through e-tivities at each stage of the model. Resources for Practitioners 5 provides many more examples and ideas.

Stage 1: Access and motivation

E-tivities at this stage need to concentrate on providing explicit motivation and set the pace and rhythm. Participants need to gain experience in the technology in use without believing it to be what the course is about! Therefore e-tivities need to be designed carefully to enable the participants to find their way around the online learning platform whilst taking part in relevant and authentic tasks.

There may be a great deal of anxiety around at this stage about how participants are expected to behave and who is online with them. This will not be visible to the e-moderator unless expressed in messages. Make a start on e-tivities that address these concerns and help people to feel more comfortable. Try to avoid the 'Post your first message here and say who you are' type of message. At the start of a conference or course such messages frighten some people, particularly the more reticent or less experienced in the online environment, and are generally unfocused and unproductive to summarize.

Stage 2: Socialization

E-tivities at stage 2 need to focus on enabling participants to relate to a few others and on reasonably stretching tasks. E-tivities at this stage should provide ways of knowing who else is in the shared space and how this knowledge can be used to guide participants' work.

Provide practice, practice and practice – not in the technology, but in working together! Stage 2 e-tivities should offer experience in developing sensitivity to gender, racial issues, potential personality conflicts and various educational values and expectations. Relate e-tivities at stage 2 to the traditions of your company, topic, discipline or profession because this provides the important cultural contexts for learning and makes later knowledge construction easier to achieve.

Stage 3: Information exchange

E-tivities at stage 3 should have a strong task and action focus. Use stage 3 e-tivities for prioritizing content, enabling participants to impart information to each other and explain and clarify. They should be shown how to provide feedback to each other in the spirit of deepening understanding. This will help them prepare to move to stage 4 e-tivities.

At stage 3 I suggest that you design e-tivities that focus on exploring co-ordination and communication between the participants so that each participant works towards his or her own objectives within the overall e-tivity. Later e-tivities at stage 3 can look towards more co-operation and support for each person's needs and objectives. In co-operation, there is more sharing of common objectives.

At this stage, you can experiment with the structure of groups and the techniques for group working. At stage 3 you will still need to be clear about which groups are assigned which parts of tasks. You could also try buzz groups (each group is given a topic) or syndicates (each group has an assigned task which culminates in a plenary debate).

Stage 4: Knowledge construction

You can increase the information that you offer as a 'spark', if you wish, after your students have become adept at working online, at managing their time and at working with each other – in other words, when they have arrived at stage 4.

Objectives at stage 4 can be related to broadening understanding, providing different viewpoints and perspectives and examples. Avoid specifying in advance exactly what has to be learnt at this point, but ground e-tivities in real-world contexts and define the processes for producing the end results required. At stage 4 you can move increasingly towards peer-directed e-tivities and participant work teams. You could try, for instance, defining a group outcome, or asking the group to provide its own goal and objectives and give directions on how to collaborate.

Discussion-based e-tivities can work well and can be used so long as they are structured and focused. Develop e-tivities that have a wide variety of interpretations and perspectives (multiple realities). Encourage dialogue and collaboration, including criticism, debate and disagreement. E-tivities can include choosing from alternatives, choosing thoughtfully (and giving reasons and arguments for choices), affirming a choice and giving proposals for improving practice and skills and acting upon choices.

Stage 5: Development

Purposes at stage 5 can be around gaining self-insight and on reflecting and making judgements on the experience and the knowledge surfaced and built.

Develop e-tivities that enable evaluation and critique of all kinds. Ask participants to demonstrate their ability to work with content and defend their own judgements. Encourage them to explore their metacognitive awareness of positions they adopt – for example, 'How did you arrive at that position?' or 'Which is better and why?' Don't forget to explore feelings and emotions about learning, as well as experience of the topics.

Resource for Practitioners 5 is the place for more ideas.

Concluding thoughts

Currently, the 'richness' of the Web depends largely on its volume and the multimedia and linked presentation of *information*. However, I believe that the key to active and interactive online teaching and learning lies in bringing us greater *interaction* and group *participation*. I believe that from these small beginnings a new body of practice will build up around e-tivities that will transfer to new technologies as they become available. The need for skilful e-moderation will not disappear, regardless of how sophisticated and fast-moving the technological environments become. E-moderators add the *real* value to learning technologies by designing and running e-tivities!

I think that the *most* successful teaching and learning organizations and associations will be those that understand, recruit, train, support and give free creative rein to their e-moderators, whilst addressing the natural fears of loss of power and perceived quality from traditional teaching staff. E-tivities will offer a key competitive advantage. E-tivities offer a subtle power because they are low cost, fun and engaging.

Part II:

RESOURCES FOR PRACTITIONERS

Designing e-tivities

Resources for practitioners 1: Designing effective e-tivities

Designing e-tivities is a creative task and might take a little more time than you think. Here is a way to start.

Start with the end in mind

What do you want to achieve by this online activity? How will it add to the participants' learning? How will you assess or evaluate the e-tivity?

First thing first!

How will you introduce and start the e-tivity off? How much notice will the participants need? Can you design clear invitational messages?

Think win: win

Why will people want to take part? Will it add obvious and clear value to their learning? How will the group work together?

Sharpen the saw

How will you prepare yourself to make this e-tivity a success? What preparation or resources will the participants need to take part?

Be proactive

Plan the e-moderator role and actions. How often will you need to intervene? What will you do about non-participants? Be realistic about the timings but be prepared to adjust them if necessary.

Seek to understand

What happens if the e-tivity doesn't go as you planned? How can you get information to change it for next time?

E-moderate

Plan what you have to do to make this all work while the e-tivity is running.

My spark for this resource is drawn from Steven Covey's seven habits of effective people and principle-centred leadership ideas (Covey, 1999).

Resources for practitioners 2: E-tivity planning

This resource offers you a simple structure for designing your e-tivities. Share your planning with a colleague!

Table II.1

Name of e-tivity	
Purpose	
Spark	
How many participants?	
Structure? Include individual response, participant responses to each other, groups and teams, plenaries	
E-lapsed time needed (be generous)	
E-moderator's time (be generous)	
E-moderator actions	
Participant time	
Participant actions	
How evaluated?	

Action notes:

Resources for practitioners 3: Building motivation into your e-tivities

- What is the extrinsic reward of taking part? Make this clear throughout each and every e-tivity.
- Are the intentions of the e-tivity clear? Do participants know exactly what's expected of them and why?
- Who will find this e-tivity easy? How can you stretch them?
- Who will find this e-tivity hard? How can you support them?
- Is the e-tivity at the right level for the whole group – will everyone see it as worthwhile?
- Who will the participants want to please by taking part? Can you build this into the e-tivity?
- Does the e-tivity need chunking up into small pieces to be more motivating? Can they cope with it all in one go?
- Are there cultural aspects that might alienate, confuse and hence demotivate some participants? How can you turn these into positive benefits?
- Is the layout of the e-tivity invitation clear? Have you proofed the message before posting it?
- What will participants lose by *not* taking part? Or by merely lurking?

Notes:

- At stages 1 and 2 do not expect intrinsic motivation to help. Be clear about the benefits.
- At stages 4 and 5 try to promote intrinsic motivators.
- Avoid 'punishment' and threats to non-participants or forced attempts at achieving contribution through assessment – they do not motivate.
- Fabulous technology and comfort with the system will only ever be a hygiene factor, not a motivator in itself.

Resources for practitioners 4: Action words for e-tivities

A list of e-tivity 'doing' words to build into your e-tivities and promote online action.

Add to
Apply
Argue
Assert
Categorize
Clarify
Classify
Comprehend
Confirm/endorse
Consider
Contribute
Debate
Demonstrate
Describe
Discuss
Draw analogy/metaphor
Elaborate
Empathize

Enumerate
Explain
Explore
Hold back
Hypothesize
Identify
Induce/deduce
Integrate
Intuit
Label
Link to
Maintain
Memorize
Mull over
Observe
Paraphrase
Provide
Question

Recast/restructure/
   re-order
Reflect
Reinforce
Relate to principle
Resolve
Seek
Show
Stroke/praise/
   compliment/support
Structure
Suggest
Summarize
Sympathize
Think
Understand

Resources for practitioners 5: Spark ideas for e-tivities

Many of these sparks for e-tivities can be used at several stages of the five-stage model. The key issue is how deeply you expect the participants to go in their responses, how much time you allow them and the e-moderator's skills at weaving and summarizing. So the level at which I've placed them is indicative only. Experiment and look carefully at outcomes!

I have given examples of spark content to make the ideas a little clearer. Many of my examples are from management or education because I am more familiar with the content of these areas. However, I am sure you will be able to see how to substitute sparks and content from your own topics, contexts, disciplines or companies.

Stage 1: Access and motivation

At this stage offer easy e-tivities that are quickly achieved while giving practice in the use of the technology. Expect to offer one-to-one help and acknowledgement to ensure positive attitudes towards the start of the experience.

If you are planning to assess the experience, process or journey of online learning, as well as outcomes, encourage regular 'point of learning' individual or group reflections from stage 1 onwards. Participants may not see the value of them at this point so will need fairly structured opportunities to reflect. However, they will set up a good spark for later use.

Icebreakers

Each of these will take around two to three weeks online. They are easy to set up and run and will enable your participants to get to know each other, to contribute rather than 'lurk', and to become more familiar with the platform in use in a fairly safe and fun way. Participants can be encouraged to find others with similar interests to share ideas with online, as well as to find learning partners who have different kinds of ideas and support to offer. With sharing and support, more serious topics and discussions go well.

Quiz

Ask each participant to put up a maximum of one screenful that reveals a little about themselves. Offer them a possible structure, such as the choice of three or four from job, home location, personal interests, family, what they hope to get out of the course, what they hope to put in, something they're good at and something they need to get better at. They could offer their learning styles or best contributions to team roles, if they know them. When every participant has contributed, set up a little quiz, based on the group, with a prize; for example, who has twin girls? Who has a spaniel dog? Who lives in XXX area? Who works in company Y as a product manager? Publicize the quiz and offer a prize (piece of software?) for the most accurate response or the fastest, or both.

Images

Ask each participant to post a URL into the conference that tells the group's members something about themselves. Put one up about yourself. Triggers might be a hobby, a personal Web site, an organizational or corporate Web site, a picture of a favourite beach, a favourite rock band, a favourite country, a favourite book, and so on. Ask each person to post a message saying why they have chosen to share their particular URL with other participants. Run this e-tivity for a week or so only and then archive it.

My brand

Ask the participants to mention a brand of something that they always use and what it says about them. Start a discussion on these brands.

Hall of mirrors

Explain how Web sites of organizations often present a more up-to-date image of them than their annual reports, brochures or other print-based publications do. Post five Web sites and call it 'The Hall of Mirrors'. Ask participants to take a wander round them and post a message saying:

- What are the similarities between the Web sites?
- Which one would encourage them to buy online and why?
- Which one would put them off buying the product or service and why?
- Which one made them feel confident and which one made them feel nervous?

Think of further questions. Allow participants, say, one week to respond, and then run a discussion on the similarities and differences in responses.

Talents

'Give' each participant a fantasy $200/$1,000/$100,000 to 'spend' online. Allow them one week to wander around the Web and say in a message what they would buy with this sum (and why). If you want to make it course related, they can investigate products that are relevant to your topic, such as online courses for educators, images for art students, and so on. Start a discussion on the different choices. Has anyone chosen to make money with their $200 rather than spend it? Who has spent it on themselves and who on others? Who has bought goods and who purchased a service?

Wanderlust

Post a URL showing a great location in your home country (for holidays or business). Ask each participant to find and post a URL showing another great location. Get each person to say what they would do or purchase on a visit to this country. Start a discussion on country specialities and global brands.

Our contract

Post a message making clear what you can offer as their e-moderator. Include number of times a week that you log on and how long you can stay online each time. Let them know any time you will be away from your computer. Indicate what your main role is; what they can expect you to do. Indicate what you would like from them. Ask participants to offer a similar message about their own commitments.

Do you get the idea? Here are some more:

- Explore the nature of success on the course.
- Each participant offers a contribution to the 'netiquette' of the group. Build a commonly agreed list of the contributions.

- Ask participants to look out of a window and relate a topic – say, critical path analysis, or leadership styles, or decision making – to natural objects such as trees or human-made objects such as traffic furniture. Go with the flow. This works!
- Offer a learning styles or team roles inventory (watch you don't infringe anyone's copyright). Ask participants to discuss their styles and how they think their styles will manifest themselves in the online environment.
- Ask participants what single thing would improve the quality of their online communication. Who could help to achieve this?
- Set up a 'skills and knowledge' market. Each participant states the help that he or she would like from one other participant. In return, they agree to help one other person.
- Set up a 'discovery' area for participants to publish their own tips and tricks on the technology. But edit it so it does not become a 'whinge' area!
- Offer key ideas (we call them 'footprints') developed by previous participants in the course. Ask new arrivals to explore the ideas.
- Ask each participant to acknowledge, congratulate or celebrate the contribution of one other participant.
- Ask participants to offer tips for 'surviving online learning'.
- Ask participants to say what they would be doing now if they weren't working online.
- Ask pairs to interview each other by e-mail and introduce each other publicly.
- Ask each person to name a famous person from their locality (town, country) and tell us one significant piece of information about this person.
- Ask participants to mention when they first received a computer on their desk or in their home, and the circumstances. When did they first hear the term 'Superhighway' or 'World Wide Web' and from whom?

Stage 2: Socialization

E-tivities at this stage are about getting to know each other, establishing a group to work with and understanding the approach that the group or community will take. Try to use humour, but watch for issues of equality that might arise from it.

There are two main kinds of e-tivity: those that appear to be about getting to know each other and those that clearly look to the work that is to come. Many participants will feel impatient with the first type so such e-tivities may need to be disguised a little. For example, one of the most successful e-tivities I have run with a very varied multicultural group was to ask about their favourite dish and why it was important to them. The discussion ran for several weeks and ranged from traditions of meals to cultural festivals. The group bonded in a rare and productive way.

Try to use innovative ways to enable participants to get to know about each other and to be able to form effective learning teams. You may think that some of these suggestions are too lightweight for adult groups. However, one or two of them, carefully chosen, will help establish the group and lead to more in-depth knowledge sharing and learning later on. The following suggestions all work.

- Introduce yourself using six descriptive words.
- What are the most popular given names in your culture? Ask each person to explain the origin of his/her name, the reason it was chosen and any special cultural significance.
- If you were an animal, what would you be? Can we make up a farmyard, zoo, circus or jungle?
- What musical instruments do you play? Can we form a band or orchestra with our skills and experience?
- Do you have any domestic pets? Why did you choose this kind of animal? What would happen if our pets met each other? How did you choose their names?
- If we were setting up a business, what could you contribute? What products would you like to make or what processes would you like to set in train?
- Give one URL that illustrates your favourite hobby.
- If you were leaving to go on holiday or a business trip what three essential items would you put in your suitcase? What kind of packer are you? Do you throw everything in and sit on the case? Do you have one or two specially selected items, carefully folded. . . or what? Compare the similarities and differences.
- What's your favourite smell? Can you describe it online? Why is it important to you?
- What's the most important lesson life/being an e-moderator/working in this company/living in this place has taught you up until now?
- How do you relax?
- Offer a cartoon or humorous picture. Ask for reactions.
- In what circumstances do you behave 'safely' and when might you take 'risks'? Can we find common categories?
- What's your favourite town? Take us on a virtual tour of it. Each participant comments on whether they have visited for real or virtually.
- What's your favourite journey? Take us along it. Start a discussion based on some feature you see along the way.
- In XXX words, what's the plot of your favourite novel? Compare and contrast the different plots.
- What items would you put in your virtual shopping basket and why? Are there similarities and differences in the group?

- What's your favourite word/expression, and why? Can we build them into a story?
- If we were to have a fancy dress party, what theme would you choose for this group? What would you come as? What periods of history/literature/continents of the world do we represent?
- Who's your favourite actor and why? Have we all chosen different people?
- Who's the person you'd most like to meet from your discipline and why? What would s/he say about working online?
- Who's the historical figure you most identify with and why? Would they like the Internet? How would they use it?
- If you were offered a soapbox, what would you talk about? Could you condense the points into 50 words?
- What's your favourite gadget and why? Will it help you communicate on this course?
- What would you like to see invented and why?
- What was your proudest moment? (Most embarrassing could be hilarious. . . but risky!)
- If I ruled the world. . .

Senses

Try to tap into issues that explore similarities and differences across cultures, learning and upbringing. Try also to include at least one e-tivity that taps into senses other than those involved in typing and reading. We have found the following especially powerful:

- My favourite music. Explore sources and roots of different kinds. Offer Web sites so participants can listen and exchange ideas.
- My favourite food. If you could live on one dish only, what would it be? What key food do you remember from your childhood? What special dishes are made in your home town?
- Online wine tasting. Each participant has a glass by his or her keyboard. They describe and discuss the taste, and the origin of the wine.
- What's the best excuse you've heard for the late submission of a piece of work that is to be assessed?
- If we were designing a physical classroom for our group, what features would be important? Where would it be located in the world and why?
- Highlight a topical issue that is relevant to your course. Ask participants to take positions as stakeholders.
- Share silly extrapolations: for example, when Elvis Presley died, there were five Elvis impersonators in the world; now there are 31,000. This means that one in 10 of us will be Elvis by 2010. How can we use such information?

Across cultures

If you have a wide variety of participants located all over the world, then you have special opportunities for exploring many aspects of diverse cultures and of globalization. You may be able to introduce these as socialization exercises at stage 2 and carry the themes and outcomes through to stages 3 and 4.

- Where is your nearest branch of Starbucks, or McDonald's? What kind of buildings or streets are around it? What conclusions can be drawn?
- Do you drive on the left or right? Why? Should it be changed?
- What are the problems and benefits of the transport systems in your country? What is the preferred mode of transport? How is it funded?
- Does your country have a national dress or costume? Have you ever worn it and when?
- Everyone contributes the words 'please' and 'thank you' or 'hello' and 'goodbye' in their mother languages. Build a list and try using them out of politeness during the course.

Scenarios

Try offering little scenarios for discussion. These can prepare groups for more demanding case studies at stage 4. For example:

- You return from a vacation. Your car is parked in the street surrounded by policemen. What has happened?
- You are responsible for marking examination papers for this course. You notice that one candidate appears to have produced answers to completely different questions to those set. What might have happened here?
- You have lived in the same apartment for 10 years. It's very quiet. Suddenly the building starts to make a noise at night. What might be happening?

At this stage, participants will probably want to see photographs of each other. Don't be in too much of a rush to offer this. Run an e-tivity on how a fixed photograph may give a stereotypical view of a participant, or of their personality or mood.

If you do go for photos at stage 2, encourage people to post several in different moods and styles, with some personal commentary.

Stage 3: Information exchange

At this stage e-tivities that can gradually encourage participants to take more personal responsibility for their active learning and interacting are helpful. In invitational messages try to suggest and model strategies for active online learning. Most participants will still need help to handle masses of response messages and to find and personalize who and what they wish to work with. The-moderator role shifts from the 'host' role at stage 2 to the archive, summarizing and feedback role at stage 3.

Great thinkers

Using the great thinkers from your disciplines can be great sparks for e-tivities. Here are some examples that we have tried:

- Offer text of great speeches. Participants condense them into 12 words and discuss the meanings.
- Suggest key concepts from your course for writing and sharing their own 'speech'.
- Ask for 'postcard' messages from one of the people from your discipline whom you admire; for example, individual explorers or inventors. How would participants respond?
- Considering the history of your discipline, are there more men or women mentioned in textbooks? Consider the implications and discuss them.
- Ask each participant to undertake a piece of research on a well-known figure. Ask participants to think of questions that they would like to ask and then to role-play interviewing each other as these figures. Try this by e-mail or through text chat. Post the results of the interviews for everyone to see.

Skills

Stage 3 is a good time and place for skill development. Try these:

- Find and try out keyboard tutors. See which increase typing speeds. Share the results of your research and see who can improve their typing speed.
- Practise summarizing information, for example the theory of relativity in 12 words.
- Practise summarizing sets of messages from stages 2 and 3.
- Undertake 'compare and contrast' research. Develop a set of criteria for good or bad sites for your course, or more or less relevant, or more or less useful. Then, using the criteria, each participant selects a Web site and indicates how he or she would evaluate it. Encourage discussion and challenge.
- Ask each participant or small group to undertake research on a topic and report back to the group. Lead a plenary discussion on the results.

Compare

Investigating and comparing and contrasting electronic resources works really well at stage 3:

- Investigate the best way for teams to work online, share ideas and evaluate them.
- If you were advising a well-known writer from your topic, what would you say about the layout and content of his/her book? What's missing? What's out of date?
- Are there any scenarios about the future for your discipline? What are they called? Who thinks they offer a likely or an unlikely view of the future?
- Ask one participant to identify three Web sites of use to the group and post an evaluation of each one. Another participant then visits each of the three sites and comments on the sufficiency of the evaluation, and adds his or her views and so on. The e-moderator summarizes.

Evaluation

Evaluation processes are usually good value for e-tivities. Try 'reversal'. What would happen if we did the opposite of what's advised by some authority? What are the 'seminal' books or papers for your areas of expertise? Why do you think they became so important?

Techniques

Try holding structured meetings to reach decisions, such as:

- political debates;
- mock board meetings;
- lobby groups;
- voting on issues;
- discussion, buzz or focus groups;
- simulations or role plays.

Take stances on key issues. For example, present a contentious issue: try 'introducing e-learning'! Divide participants into five groups; for example, student sceptics, teacher sceptics, wild enthusiasts (students), serious enthusiasts (teachers), pragmatists (it's going to happen, so how will we do it?). Run a plenary taking the key issues from each, and solutions.

Creative techniques

Here are some creative techniques:

- brainstorming;
- Delphi techniques;
- nominal group techniques;
- reversal;
- metaphors.

Creativity

Promote 'out-of-the-box' thinking.

- Imagine that better treatment for human bones and joints means that walking (Zimmer) frames are no longer needed. What could we do with all the Zimmer frames in the world?
- Try cybernetics (comparisons between human-made and biological objects). Offer a topic, then each participant types examples of five items from his or her desk. Try to 'force-fit' connections and see if they offer new insights into the topic.
- Start a 'round robin' story. Start by offering two sentences relevant to your course. Each participant adds a sentence.

Questions

Try posting intriguing questions from any relevant topic of your choice. Or try to choose something that is simply one word or phrase. It works best if there are many different interpretations and perhaps a movie or Internet sites to explore. You will need very good summaries when the questions are answered and a plenary to explore the meaning and usefulness of the information.

For example, we asked these about the word 'Titanic':

- Where do we get valid information from?
- Why was there such a belief in the unsinkable nature of the *Titanic*?
- How many people did a lifeboat hold (and why)?
- Where did the *Titanic* sail from?
- What kind of people were on board?
- Has the *Titanic* been raised from the sea?
- How many people survived the disaster? What kind of people were they?
- How many movies have been made about the sinking of the *Titanic*?
- What does the word 'Titanic' mean?

- Who holds the rights to the sunken treasure?
- Who directed the film *Raise the Titanic*?
- Where is the *Titanic* Museum?
- What was the name of the character that Kate Winslett played in one *Titanic* film?
- Did the captain go down with the ship?
- Who rescued the survivors?

Try getting participants to brainstorm questions as well as answers too.

Visitors

From stage 3 onwards, you might want to introduce selective use of an 'outsider' such as topic expert to the group to stimulate discussion. To maximize the use of their time, build them into e-tivity processes and be specific about what you want them to do and when! Ask participants to practise their questioning and summarizing skills.

Stage 4: Knowledge construction

Your participants should be working well together by this point.

Structured teams

You can start to run 'snowball'-type e-tivities, with smaller groups merging into bigger ones. You can explore structures of effective work teams and specific roles such as chair, resource finder, recorder, summarizer, reviewer, critic and time-keeper. Try some action learning sets for e-tivities with participant-led e-moderating and team leading.

Concepts

At this stage in a course or process, it's important to introduce conceptual models, ideas and theories for examination, exploration and application. In e-tivity processes, make it clear that the e-moderator is not necessarily looking for consensus or closure, but wide exploration of issues:

- Take a key diagram, model or concept from your course or discipline. Ask each participant to apply it, or find examples. Compare and contrast between the examples offered.

- Take a key concept and apply it in a new way.
- Take a key concept and demonstrate the extent to which it does or does not apply to a particular case example.

Positions

Participants can very usefully adopt a variety of 'positions' online to cover multiple perspectives. Here are some ideas:

- Take a key concept or model and explore how people belonging to different professions, such as that of physician, lawyer, politician or teacher, would apply it.
- Cases: case studies and problem-based learning work well at this point.
- Introduce staged case-study information with questions.
- Introduce challenging problems with a variety of solutions.
- Ask participants to produce plans for action based on limited amounts of information, for example a marketing plan, a business plan, a product launch.
- Use scenarios for the future. Offer two or three different cameos of how your discipline will look in the future, for example different types of schools, new technologies for medicine, virtual performing arts. Prompt discussion on the adequacy and implications of these scenarios.

Summarizing

Encourage all forms of reviewing and summarizing:

- Ask individual participants, teams or groups to undertake investigation of one topic or area to contribute to a whole piece of work or report.
- Ask individual participants, teams or groups to undertake summarizing, critiquing and combining information.
- Offer e-tivities that rework ideas or discussions using techniques such as concept mapping.

Stage 5: Development

At this stage try to allow the maximum amount of choice. Ensure that all the summaries and archives are available for participants to use as resources. Accountability and responsibility are more important at this stage than 'content'. However, the usual approach to pacing and timescales should continue.

At this stage, I've suggested sparks that focus on self-reflection and evaluation of the learning. However many of these approaches can also be used for teacher- or peer-led assessment. Almost all of them can form part of a written report or essay that can be used for assessment. In this way the maximum amount of 'alignment' between learning and assessment can be achieved.

Footprints

Offer essays or reports from previous students on the course (with permission or disguised, of course) and run an e-tivity on how participants would have marked, assessed and graded them.

Review

Offer e-tivities to consider the evaluation of both the learning that has occurred and the knowledge that has been generated:

- Try 360-degree evaluation or assessment – each participant asks another three participants specific questions about their experience of working together. Encourage participants to explore how they judge their success.
- Go back to expectations at the beginning of the course. Would participants change them if starting again? To what extent have their expectations been met and why?
- Would the group have worked differently if it had met physically too? If so, in what way?

Technology

Explore the technology in use:

- If the group were designing an online environment, what would it need?
- What one new feature in the technology would have helped with learning?
- How did the participants succeed in spite of a barrier created by the technology?

Reflections

Encourage reflection on the overall experience:

- Ask participants to review one of their own messages and rework it to show how they would like it to appear now.

- Try asking for examples of various concepts to be picked out, or summaries or further conclusions to be drawn from earlier e-tivities.
- Ask for action plans – offer some structure and feedback.
- Ask for personal development plans – offer some structure and feedback.
- Give masses of feedback and constructive criticism. Encourage participants to offer this to each other too.
- Ask individuals and groups to offer a 'footprint' (a piece of knowledge, new idea, special insight) to be offered to others starting the course afresh. Ask groups to agree the footprint statement between them.
- Ask participants to review all posted messages and to comment on what helped to move the discussion along and what did not.
- Ask participants to comment on the roles they each adopted.
- Ask participants to articulate the emotions they felt at various points in the course, and why.

If developing skills in reflection is a purpose, you could try collecting these up:

Ask each participant to summarize from their perspective what transpired during the e-tivity for him or her. Then they e-mail the summary to you as the e-moderator. After you've received them all, you can (with their permission) summarize and post them into a group area and ask them to discuss their respective perspectives and interpretations. At this point, either individual or group writing for assessment could take place. BL

If your participants understand a concept or topic better because of taking part in an e-tivity, you'll find that they will express satisfaction in the experience in some way. Try asking them what they would do differently as a result of taking part in the e-tivities (Wiske, 1998) as a form of assessment. You can also build this kind of self-assessment into an e-tivity. Some learning platforms offer the opportunity to embed feedback quizzes and tests into e-tivities. These can be useful to start an e-tivity off as a spark for discussion, or to give occasional fast feedback to participants as part of regular pacing.

Developing e-tivities

Resources for practitioners 6: Building programmes and processes with e-tivities

One, two, three or more e-tivities can be used within any kind of learning programmes, blended with other methods and techniques of teaching or combined with other online resources in a wide variety of ways. In the Open University, online tutorials and seminars are commonly used to replace face-to-face meetings of students, or in addition to them. E-tivities work well and are enjoyed by students if combined with lectures on a university campus. The large business school at Glasgow Caledonian University in Scotland is pioneering this approach for undergraduates.

This resource offers three examples of putting a series of e-tivities together within the framework of the five-stage model. The only limits are those of your own imagination.

Example 1 shows an entirely online course, or one with only the minimum of supplied resources, such as a book. Here, four e-tivities are offered each week and the cohort of participants is expected to finish the set of e-tivities at the end of each week and move on together to the next week.

Participants need to log on several times a week to take part successfully. The course described in Chapter 3 is based on a model similar to this one.

Example 2 shows a more intensive course, where participants take part in short e-tivities for two weeks, experience a face-to-face seminar and then go back online for further work and e-tivities, applying the ideas and reflecting on the learning. They are expected to offer around six hours online in the first two weeks, meet for seven hours and then go on line for a further three. They then undertake around six hours' work to write up their experience.

Example 3 (Figure II.1) shows a course based on a 12-week university or college semester, with a one-week 'catch-up' break two-thirds of the way through. Here most e-tivities last around two weeks, and the stages overlap each other. Participants need to commit around three hours per week online.

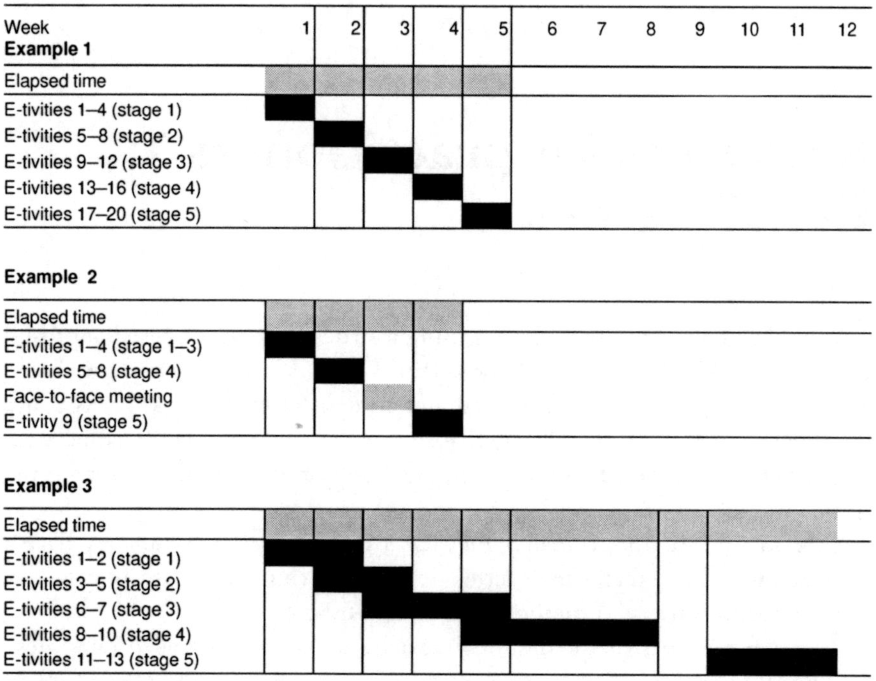

Figure II.1

Resources for practitioners 7: E-mail games

You might like to try out e-tivities using a structured games-based approach using e-mail. Marie Jasinski and Sivasailam 'Thiagi' Thiagarajan run text-based asynchronous games through e-mail and asynchronous forums (Jasinski and Thiagarajan, 2000). Marie tells me that she and Thiagi have played games with over 2,500 people worldwide. But you need only around 10 players for a game to be productive.

Like many e-tivities, e-mail games use a playful approach but they have a serious intent. All e-mail games have a learning purpose. They are an easy way of introducing variety of method into your e-tivities.

E-mail games are structured through text-based frameworks called 'templates'. A template provides a guide to a series of actions or 'rounds' for groups of participants and e-moderators and so form the process of the e-game.

The role of e-moderators is to orchestrate the games. They select a template, adapt it to suit the context, collate content, facilitate each round of play and debrief the participants on the process after the game is over.

Marie and Thiagi use the approach of inviting colleagues to use the templates in return for sharing their results and modifications. Their openness and sharing encourages adoption and rapid improvement of e-games e-tivities. You can find some sample templates at Thiagi's Web site at www.thiagi.com.

Here are two examples of e-mail games.

Game 1: Half-life

The purpose of this game is to identify and synthesize the critical elements of a concept, topic, product, procedure or issue. During the game, players analyse the content and synthesize the key elements into progressively shorter sentences.

This e-mail game consists of five rounds. Here's a summary of the template for each round, with a sample response from a player:

Round 1. 'How do you keep online learners on track?' Write a response to this question in exactly 32 words (no more, no less).
Sample response:

> An initial personal welcoming e-mail would be addressed to each student, encouraging direct e-mail contact with the regularly responsive e-moderator. The e-moderator's availability at set times on the Web board should be highlighted.

Round 2. Read the 32-word responses from different players to the question 'how do you keep online learners on track?' Write a response to the question in exactly 16 words. Sample response:

> To best keep online learners on track, e-moderators must be responsive, available, supportive, empathetic, proactive motivators.

Round 3. Read the 16-word responses to the question 'how do you keep online learners on track?' Now write a response in exactly eight words. Sample response:

> Responsive, supportive, empathetic, proactive e-moderators motivate online learners.

Round 4. Read the eight-word responses to the question: 'how do you keep online learners on track?' Now write a response in exactly four words. Sample response:

> Inspiring e-moderators energize learners.

Round 5. Read the four-word responses to the question: 'how do you keep online learners on track?' Now write a response in exactly two words. Sample response:

> Empathize, inspire.

Game 2: C3PO

C3PO stands for *challenge, pool, poll, predict, outcome*. The purpose of this e-mail game is collaborative problem solving. Here is an overview of how the game is played.

In round 1 of C3PO, players receive an open-ended challenge (in this example, it was 'how do you increase person-to-person interaction in Internet-based training?'). Each player sends the e-moderator three ideas to meet this challenge.

In round 2, the e-moderator sends the resulting pool of ideas back to the players and asks them to generate a priority list. Players read through the pool of ideas, select the three that personally appeal to them most, and send them to the e-moderator.

In round 3, players review the same pool of ideas, make a prediction of how the entire group would have voted and identify the top three that would have received the most votes.

So during round 2, the players consider how they personally feel and react to the ideas. During round 3 the players put themselves in other players' positions and predict the reaction of the population. As one player put it, 'The prediction step forces you to stop thinking wishfully, projecting your preferences, and become absolutely objective.'

The player with the closest prediction is the winner. After the results have been announced, players participate in an online forum to debrief each other and analyse the game. They also have a useful list of tips for increasing person-to-person interaction in Internet-based training.

Here is the final list of top tips generated when this game was played with a group of e-moderators in Australia. The list was published as a resource for colleagues to use.

- Use a range of activities. Combine Internet interaction with other activities, such as telephone conversation, face-to-face discussion with peers, and real-world application exercises.
- Address key questions. Make sure that the content and the activities directly address the participants' question 'What's in it for me?'
- Be user-friendly. Make the interaction procedure as simple and straightforward as possible.
- Ensure that technology is usable. Make sure that all participants have access to, and know how to use, the Internet, e-mail and all other tools you will be using.
- Ask better questions. Use relevant and provocative open-ended questions and require responses from participants.
- Require interaction. Ensure that everyone understands that participant interaction is required. Also, explain the importance of such interaction.

- Support teamwork. Require small teams of participants to collaboratively answer questions to solve problems.
- Respond quickly. Immediately and enthusiastically acknowledge each participant's posting, especially the first ones to appear.
- Build confidence. Make participants feel safe and secure by permitting anonymous postings, if desired.
- Be personal. Use a conversational style.
- Provide rewards. Provide prizes and inexpensive rewards for outstanding participation.

Debriefing is offered by the e-moderator after every game. Debriefing provides the opportunity for participants to come together to draw out learning points, share experiences, discuss processed content and bring the game to closure.

Marie uses Thiagi's six-stage debriefing model to trigger discussion about different types of experiences:

- *How do you feel?* This gives participants an opportunity to get any emotions off their chest so it's easier for them to be objective in the later phases.
- *What happened?* This encourages participants to compare and contrast their experiences and recollections and to draw general conclusions.
- *What did you learn?* This question encourages participants to generate and test different hypotheses and to raise and discuss general principles.
- *How does this relate to the real world?* During this stage participants discuss the relevance of the experience to real-world contexts.
- *What if?* Participants share and apply insights to new concepts and speculate on how outcomes could change had different variables been introduced.
- *What next?* This is the action-planning phase that allows participants to apply their insights to the real world.

Marie and Thiagi have found that the depth of debriefing required for e-mail games depends on the nature of the game, the topic in question and the group of participants. A brainstorming game may need minimal debriefing, whereas a role-play game may require more focused debriefing to tease out the learning points. Like any experiential e-tivity, e-mail games can be unpredictable. A debriefing framework allows e-moderators to be both flexible and yet prepared for whatever may emerge.

If you are interested in participating in a game, contact Marie at mariejas@ bigpond.com.

Resources for practitioners 8:
Creativity and e-tivities

Why should we try to be more creative and inventive in our e-tivities? Here is the response from one e-moderator:

> Many of our participants have experienced many courses, presentations and seminars and are used to skimming documents. We often now want them to learn in more depth. However expecting people to concentrate in front of a computer over weeks, month and years is expecting a lot! Without the sense of fun, the sense of otherness, the sense of standing back, participants will only learn tips and tricks. But with the sense of wonder, they can change the way they think and work. As e-moderators we have to help create and sustain the sense of wonder. IW

This resource offers an overview of thinking and acting differently in the context of developing and e-moderating e-tivities. The idea is to introduce more fun and freedom into your e-tivities. A 'touch of creativity' in our e-tivities and our e-moderating work will delight our participants and we'll all have more fun.

By example and by influence, e-moderators can enable online participants to think and act more creatively, which is a most important attribute for everyone in the fast-changing 21st century. What better way to take part in the 21st century's new skills than to learn online how to succeed in a networked world? Solving problems and innovating are unlikely to be successful if based on what worked in the past. We can model ways of doing things differently in our e-tivities and keep our teaching dynamic at the same time.

Thinking creatively involves breaking down and restructuring knowledge in order to secure new insights. Understanding how we have created that knowledge in our minds in the first place helps us to reorganize our thoughts.

The easiest way to start is by trying some techniques and learning for yourself. The only rule is that you need to take a little controlled risk from time to time. Preparation, however, is just as important as always. However, you might need to be sanguine about the precise outcome that you achieve. Go with the flow!

Creative thinking involves two main kinds of processes: divergent and convergent. Divergent thinking involves widening the thought processes around a specific issue and generating many ideas. To encourage divergent thinking it is important to remove constraints and structures and push away the usual boundaries. When the limits of divergent thinking seem to be reached, convergence can narrow down the possibilities and choices can be made. Convergent and divergent processes map closely onto the way we often design e-tivities. For example, we ask each participant to contribute some experience or an idea, we ask the group to keep building on them, then later we ensure that they are grouped or categorized and explored or explained in the plenary.

Here are some sparks for you to explore.

Images

Gareth Morgan, writing about metaphors and imaging, says, 'We are often trapped by the images we hold of ourselves' (Morgan, 1993). If we reconsider the image we have of ourselves with others, our colleagues, our participants, other stakeholders in e-tivities, and in a creative learning environment, we can break open the traps. We can create shared meanings and new ways of understanding and working with ideas. We can give energy and focus to the task of teaching and learning.

There is a story about a group of climbers who became badly lost in a severe snowstorm in Switzerland. They had nearly given up hope when one person found a map in his pocket. The group summoned up the last of their energy and found their way to safety. Only later was it discovered that the map was of the Pyrenees, not the Alps!

Where does your map of teaching and learning online come from? Has it been influenced by poor experiences as a learner or an online participant? Who or what was the most influence on creating your map of the way e-moderating works? Will it get you out of trouble or does it lead you constantly down new and exciting paths? What kind of impression will it give to others when you are in an online group?

Metaphors

Metaphors in e-tivities give insights into everyday processes. These often lead to new ideas. We can use metaphors as sparks in e-tivities. They also work well in summaries to offer new insights to participants.

Here is a metaphor from one e-moderator. He was simultaneously taking part in one of our five-week courses to increase his e-moderating skills (see Chapter 3) and tutoring on an online MA course.

I think the following metaphor applies to my online experience during the last month. The e-mod course has been like being lifted in a balloon on a clear day, with perfect weather conditions, so as to gain a colourful and friendly view of the e-moderating landscape. Now, my MA course is like having to be one of the pilots on a transatlantic flight, needing to monitor carefully very sophisticated signals for the take-off and to ensure that everyone would feel confident enough that we would land safely 8 months later having enjoyed an enriching long-term learning experience. Two very different contexts and time frames. Both challenging and valuable in their own ways. I wonder if I can introduce a balloon to the jet flight? PG

Here are some metaphors that Open University tutors have suggested give them new insights into the e-moderating role:

The e-moderator as a football club manager

I've always thought of a football club manager when I think of the e-moderator's role. First of all, you have to get out on the coaching ground (the Web) and run some regular varied routines which develop new skills in your players (e-tivities). In between times you have to motivate the players (participants) through all their problems, and cope with those niggling little injuries when they can't seem to get the assessment on time.

Second, you have to deal with the whole team, from your expensive signings (those participants with lots of ability), your youth team products (the young students with lots of potential or those of any age new to online) and the free transfers (participants you may have doubts about but who get through somehow).

Third, you have to motivate the players (participants) after matches (e-tivities and assignments). You can praise those who've done well (carefully online), encourage those who've done reasonably (to bring out the best in them), and gently let those who've done badly know what they need to do to make the grade in this league.

Fourth, you have to deal with TV and the media (the writers and producers of the course and the e-tivities), who are continually looking for feedback and may not have experienced what it's like to play a team from the lower divisions (run an e-tivities with failing software), or to play a team stuffed full of internationals, unfamiliar with the home team's cultural ideas (inter-cultural course).

Fifth, you have to listen to the chairman (the monitor). Good monitors (like good chairmen of football clubs) don't second-guess what you do but do give helpful words of advice – which you need to listen to and take account of. They stay in the background and don't interfere too much but give timely advice. Bad chairmen (and monitors) always want to interfere and pick the team for you.

And finally, you yourself have to keep up to date with the latest developments in the game and in coaching (your subject, your e-moderating skills). You have to stand on cold, windswept terraces watching reserves for that jewel for the future (i.e. scour the journals for articles and write-ups that you can use as spark). PS

Financial investment

As e-moderators we have relatively little face-to-face contact with participants, compared with a conventional teaching situation. We compensate with e-tivities, assignments, e mail and telephone contact. So we have to maximize our effectiveness at these moments. Participants will, on their own, read the course and understand a good deal of it. Our added value as e-moderators is to every so often test their understanding, help bring out the true issues, consolidate what has been learnt, question the theory. This is putting a little money aside every so often, providing added value at a good moment in a useful way. Thus I see my role of weaving, archiving and summarizing as the interest on their investment. KL

Chrysalis to butterfly

At the beginning of the course, participants emerge from the chrysalis (of logging on), blinking around in the light. At first, participants flit all over the garden (platform) and the e-moderator's role is to enable them to fly in formation towards flowers of knowledge at particular times (e-tivities) and then, looking splendid, wings furled, go into the exam! Thereafter the life cycle begins again. . . SG

Online groups as choirs

Choirs have to be coached and taught how to read music (stages 1 and 2 of the model). They need very regular rehearsals (e-tivities). Some sing only in a group, others are solo artists (issues of participation, lurking, vicarious learning). They need at stages 3 and 4 to work together. In the end they give a wonderful final performance and have all enjoyed the experience (stage 5). (Yes – some do sing out of tune, and some very flat!) JA

Piggy banks

I see the mind of a participant as a piggy bank. There is a slot for ideas, experiences, concepts, suggestions to enter (through taking part in e-tivities). Sometimes they will enter easily; sometimes it may be necessary to ease the slot open a little: to take larger coins, perhaps from another country, or folded notes, in the event of real riches (contingent e-moderating). Getting things out may also be a varied experience. Sometimes there is a lock and a little key, which can be fine if we have not lost the key. Others have a little plastic snap-on cover which we may need to prise off carefully. If this doesn't work, we may need to use a tool. If that is no good either, we may need someone else to help us. Having travelled that route, we may then reflect on how much easier it would have been if we had asked for some help a little earlier (role of emotions and time).

Sometimes there may seem to be no apparent way of extracting the contents at all. Then we may need to go back to the slot and see if we can slip something in there which can be used to ease things out again (IT help?). Or, we may need to try and create a totally new way in, so that all the goodies inside can flow out freely (revamp the e-tivity). If we do not want everything to cascade out all at once, we may need to fit a tap or two; or perhaps a little door, and for this one, we will look after the key carefully (managing contribution). PC

Knowledge circulation

I find it helps to picture knowledge as a circulatory system, rather like the human blood circulation system. The components of blood are many and varied, and derive from a number of sources. Some of these are internal, such as hormones (contributions from other participants), some of them external, such as food (spark and Web sites). Knowledge enters into the bloodstream in a similar way. If things are not going well, attempts may be made to inject the knowledge (give additional, information, assess). It circulates around with pumps to help (the e-moderator!) and serves a critical life-giving purpose for the person concerned. GK

Can you try metaphors in your e-tivities?

Another common way to stimulate ideas is to consider objects that encapsulate or represent activities, ideas and processes.

Mission to Mars

Now imagine that the president or leader of your country has just e-mailed you and asked you to put together a box of artefacts that represent e-moderating in 2003 (a key feature of any economy on earth!). This box is to be sent on the next mission to Mars. What would you put in it? What would your response be?

Here are some ideas that e-moderators have given me:

- a warm welcome message;
- an e-tivity or other learning object;
- some icons;
- a short message sequence;
- a diskette of prepared material;
- some screen pictures;
- pictures of people in front of screens.

This idea also works well as a stage 2 e-tivity. You can also ask your participants to draw their objects and send them into the conferences as an attachment. They should also justify their choices to each other. For example, try it with key issues of the year from your discipline, or this week's news from around the world.

Reversal

By turning a situation or problem around and looking at it differently, we often get fresh and interesting new perspectives or ideas. A frequently used creative technique is 'reversal'. For example, try 'How can we make group e-tivities more boring?'

Here are some ideas:

- always lecture, don't involve others in activities;
- never make your objectives clear;
- single individuals out and demand answers to your questions;
- don't virus-check;
- talk endlessly about your own experience without relating it back to the concepts in the course;
- intervene regularly, and answer your own messages.

Did you think of many others?

Now take your list and reverse the ideas – you have a simple list of good practice. For example:

- plan activities and involvement of everyone;
- ensure the online environment is suitable and have plenty of pacing and breaks;
- be clear about outcomes expected, timings and process;
- support the group process as a whole, avoiding unnecessary interventions;
- use only appropriate and clear teaching sparks, links and references;
- plan examples and illustrations carefully.

Do you get the idea? You could try reversal and then re-reversal now: 'How can we ensure that novice computers users do not become fully comfortable with electronic learning?' and 'How can we use assignment marking to undermine students' confidence?'

Can you try out one of these ideas with your participants in one of your e-tivities? Make a note of how you felt about trying this and what the participants' responses were. Could you see the divergent and convergent phase? Most importantly, can you see whether they were thinking a little differently, a little more creatively than usual? Were they all fully engaged in the task? Did they comment on their own ways of learning as well as the outcome from the task?

Resources for practitioners 9: Promoting collaborative groups

When groups of learners get together, they nearly always exchange views and ideas. We know that people enjoy learning from the experiences of others as well as from provided resources such as Web sites and books. A key learning skill is shaping and achieving goals in learning sets or work teams. To offer these benefits, within any learning programme, a considerable amount of 'group work' needs to be included.

Traditionally, group work has been carried out with small face-to-face groups led by a tutor or instructor and hence often called 'tutorials'. The challenge is to ensure this happens equally well, or better, in online encounters. E-tivities are the online equivalent of tutorials.

As you will have read so far, the ideas of e-tivities are based largely on participants 'making sense' of material through interaction with their peers and with their e-moderators. This is why I always suggest that each e-tivity, at all stages of the model, includes a response to the messages of others to start to build participation. Groups do not find it easy to work virtually (Rossen, 2001) so without careful structuring, it is unlikely that discussion will move beyond, at best, sharing of information, support and encouragement.

As Chapter 2 suggests, it is important to gradually establish group working through the stages of the model. More in-depth learning in groups is then likely to happen through groups at stages 3 and 4. A broad distinction can be made between co-operative working (the group help each other towards individual goals) and collaborative working (often linked with practice or knowledge construction, working together towards a group goal). Co-operation is often the aim at stage 3 of the model, and collaboration at stage 4.

Collaboration requires an active sharing of information and *intellectual* resources amongst the participants. The best experience of collaboration by participants for learning purposes enables them to experience both personal, individualistic, useful learning whilst contributing to a community of learners and the support and development of others. E-moderators should never underestimate the resources that they work with: participants *can* comprehend, evaluate, debate, question, integrate and synthesize information online, with suitable e-tivities and ongoing support. One of the best ways of encouraging collaboration is around a highly invitational group task. Not only may assessment be linked to the group's individual learning outcome, but both intrinsic and extrinsic rewards may be given for the group processes achieved and for the quality and level of individual contributions. It may be possible to encourage the group to identify outcomes and assessment criteria and processes for itself.

Over 100 theoretical models of group development can be explored. They all include four main key characteristics: *forming, control, work process* and *ending*. One of the commonest in regular use is Tuckman's forming, storming, norming, performing (Tuckman and Jenson, 1977; Tuckman, 1965). The five-stage online process is intended to produce a scaffold of gradually increasing comfort with working successfully together *online*. Some e-moderators find it helpful to explain the characteristics of successful team roles (such as Belbin's (1981)) and ensure that the main roles in the group are adopted, such as chairing or convening, recording and timekeeping.

The e-moderator's role is to suggest the purpose of the learning process and provide the environment to enable collaboration to take place in optimum conditions (rather than to do any of the collaborative work). With less experienced groups, it may be helpful, or necessary, for the e-moderator to set clear targets and deadlines for the completion of sets of e-tivities and outputs, or to allow very much more time for the student group to work these out.

From stage 4 onwards, e-moderators can design e-tivities that:

- create, define and identify a problem or opportunity associated with the desired learning outcome (eg working with a case study, analysing a situation, designing a product);
- identify team roles (though not necessarily allocating them);
- involve the team or group working *together* to designing analytical or other research evaluation or enquiry activities and carrying them out;
- involve the collaborative team making choices and decisions;
- involve the collaborative team creating and defending a plan or an action list;
- involve the collaborative team presenting the outcomes to others outside the group, preferably through an online environment, and defending them;
- make appropriate time and space for reviewing and evaluating the learning.

Allow plenty of elapsed time for such processes.

To be a successful e-moderator of collaborative groups, you need to:

- be able to plan structured and paced e-tivities;
- be able to run successful e-tivities;
- be able to value and enhance contribution from all members of your learning groups;
- be able to choose and deploy a wide range of techniques for group working in a purposeful way;
- be able to appreciate and deploy understandings of sharing of knowledge, co-operation, collaboration;
- be able to weave and summarize contributions to e-tivities.

Resources for practitioners 10: Autotelic e-tivities

As you gain experience and confidence in creating and e-moderating your e-tivities, you might also be a little more ambitious. At this point, some e-moderators tend to rush off for more multi-media content, or a better platform, or larger numbers. Of course, those ideas may be very valuable. However, adding a little more 'magic' to your e-tivities might also be worth trying, especially as participants become experienced (and enthusiastic) in working online and the role of the technology less important.

You could consider the concept of autotelism. Autotelic theories derive from Csikszentmihalyi's (1988) studies of enjoyment and the conditions that underlie it. Autotelism originally described creative processes such as making music or more physical activities such as sports. Csikszentmihalyi researched creating 'flow' – which derives from unconscious value deriving from the experience itself. Flow suggests a state that generates pleasure, gratification and intrinsic motivation for the participant. We are familiar with how this works in a successful face-to-face group – we sense the 'buzz' and participants often tell us how much they *enjoyed* taking part.

More recently, researchers have been applying these ideas to computing (Ghani and Deshpande, 1995) and to teaching and learning (Gammon and Lawrence, 2000). Online, the aim is that participants become similarly immersed in the experience and forget about problems (such as the technology). They lose 'self-consciousness' and feel part of the ongoing online group or community.

These are my suggestions for the seven conditions for autotelic e-tivities:

- **Challenging activity that requires skill.** The best e-tivities are those that are stretching, worthwhile and active. They need to generate a sense of mastery and engagement in the participants. Think carefully about challenging outcomes for your e-tivities but allow sufficient time for participants to be successful.

- **Merging of awareness and action.** You will observe that some participants in e-tivities become deeply involved in the online action and interaction – others less so. Try to encourage those who do become involved to partner those who are less enthusiastic for appropriate support.

- **Clear goals and feedback.** After you have run an e-tivity a few times, you will know what works and be able to offer clearer goals and more effective feedback on achievement by participants. Encourage them to create their own goals and feedback too.

- **Concentration on the task in hand.** Make the task as relevant as possible and promote the interaction. Check back constantly with participants how they are feeling (not just how they are thinking!). The idea of authentic and useful tasks will help here. Ensure that the group is well socialized and integrated at stage 2 before moving on to stage 3.

- **Paradox of control.** This is a complicated concept but one that I think applies well to the paradoxes of working online. What participants need most is not a sense of being in control, but of exercising control in difficult circumstances and of moving away from safe routines. The scaffolding of the five-step model allows for this increasing sense of mastery. So it is important to ensure that e-tivities continue to be stretching and appropriate as the participants move up through the stages, and that participants are gradually encouraged to be more self determined. Try to make e-tivities interesting and worthwhile in themselves, diverting participants away from constant attention to assessment.

- **Loss of self-conciousness.** Autotelism suggests that when we cease to be self-focused, we have a chance to expand our ideas of who we are. Working online in diverse groups promotes self-reflection and widens understandings. It is therefore worthwhile designing e-tivities that explore expanding concepts of identity, such as using creative techniques or borrowing ideas from other disciplines. Such e-tivities can easily be offered from stage 2 onwards. Resources for Practitioners 5 offers many ideas.

- **Transformation of time.** One of the commonest aspects of autotelism is a different experience of time passing compared to clock watching! Csikszentmihalyi suggests 'freedom from the tyranny of time'. We know that online, time takes on a quite different construct. Sometimes, people are amazed how long they have been online because they have been so involved (not always because the technology is slow!). At stages 4 and 5 of the model, we should encourage participants to 'go with the flow of time' and take what time they need and can, to benefit most from the experience.

Autotelic e-moderating

Here are my suggestions for autotelic e-moderating:

- Visualize success for individuals and the group, and engage with them in achieving the vision.
- Turn apparent threats into challenges to be tackled as worthwhile tasks in themselves.
- Create focus for the group by offering short-term goals and give a lot of constructive feedback.
- Give very close attention to group processes, but avoid constant interventions and redirections.
- From stage 4 onwards, promote the experience of 'going with the flow'. Most people have some sense of what this might mean. Encourage participants to articulate feelings of engagement with the e-tivities.

Resources for practitioners 11: Online emotions

There are many factors involved in personal abilities that contribute to learning and achieving. One major aspect is known as emotional quotient (EQ) (Goleman, 1996). Emotions and more unconscious aspects of learning need to be given time to develop (Claxton, 1997). It is worthwhile trying to promote an increase in EQ in your participants through your e-tivities, as the online groups will achieve more, and more comfortably.

Working online creates a wide range of feelings in participants and in e-moderators. Frustration with the technology is common but this is often soon forgotten. The experience of not physically being with others in the same space is probably the main emotions trigger. Isolation has two dimensions. One is distance in place (being alone) and psychological (distance in thoughts, feeling alone).

Features of high EQ include:

- self-awareness;
- management of the emotions;
- self-motivation;
- the ability to read the emotions of others;
- handling relationships (without being subsumed by them) – for example, making personal connections, being good at defusing explosive situations;
- taking time for reflection (Claxton, 1997).

Here are some ideas for e-moderators:

- Set up simple rules at the beginning to take care of 'feelings'.

- These can include always acknowledging feelings and offering support.
- Don't forget to include yourself.
- Base future decisions of group processes on principles that take account of holistic emotional needs, not just given learning objectives.
- If things go particularly well or badly, draw the group's attention immediately to the reasons – the consequences of actions.
- Recognize your need as an e-moderator to work out and systematize your responses to common online emotional issues.
- Keep all online responses in polite and measured tones to avoid inflaming feelings unnecessarily.

Working with online emotions

Online, emotions may be expressed different ways. Some are explicit and some more subtle.

Emoticons

happy :-)   sad :-(a wink ;-)

Describe the emotion in words

- I felt uncomfortable when. . .
- I just can't believe I was offline when you replied so quickly to my news. . .
- When I read about your achievement, I felt I had to congratulate you. . .
- I was sad to hear that. . . it reminded me of when I. . .

Describe your body language

- When I read your message, I jumped for joy!
- I smiled when I read about. . .
- Ha Ha, I said out loud!
- Mmmmm. . .walking about wondering about that. . .

Developing atunement to text-expressed emotions

- Lots of punctuation marks!!!!!!, CAPITAL LETTERS or short sentences suggest a rapid and possibly angry response.

- Sentences that start by denying a feeling, such as 'I'm not sexist but. . .', 'I'm not easily upset but. . .' sometimes mean the opposite.
- A direct challenge in the form of a question (rather different from exploratory questions) –for example, 'didn't you promise that. . .?', 'haven't you heard the research that proves. . .?' – may suggest irritation.
- Some people become annoyed and distracted by typos and spelling mistakes in messages, especially if they are unused to online communication, and express indignation.

Emotions can be expressed through:

- short messages suggesting a prompt response, indicative of a sense of excitement and shared joy;
- use of words or phrases with exclamation marks both in message titles and in the body of the message, for example 'brilliant!' 'wham!' 'fab news!' 'congratulations!'
- use of emoticons, for example (((((0)))) (this means a hug);
- references to actions and body language such as 'jumped for joy'; 'clapped my hands';
- references to ongoing relationship and interest, for example 'interested in your findings', 'can I help?'
- careful use of words, often describing body language: 'fantastic news, well done', 'when I read your email I gave such a yahoo!'
- being more 'economical', or humorous: 'I've just read your e-mail about the research grant. Congratulations! Well done!' or 'I wish I had an unsend button. I do value your contribution to this project and hope that that you accept my apology and that we can get back to the good working relationship we had.'

Some words for expressing emotions:

special	wow	congratulations
well done	great	fantastic
reward	hard work	tell me more
celebrate	thrilled	significant
recognize		

Negative emotions can be expressed by use of exclamations and emoticons and apologies (sincere to downright grovelling).

Key strategies for defusing negative emotions:

- 'I could be entirely wrong – it has been known!';
- apology combined with self-deprecation;
- apology combined with question – rhetorical or otherwise;
- positive compliment and/or sentiment about continued positive relationship;
- fairly blunt affirmation and use of negative feelings to reinforce the message.

Resources for practitioners 12: More intelligent e-tivities

As you get into the swing of developing and running e-tivities, you may want to start to look at them more creatively. But try to avoid making them longer! Instead, start to think of putting the pieces together. This is one way to view the term 'intelligence': to mean the use of wisdom, insight, intuition and experience (MacGilchrist, Myers and Reed, 1997). I've borrowed from MacGilchrist's ideas in *The Intelligent School* for the list that follows.

Here are some ideas to stimulate your thinking about e-tivities:

- *Contextual intelligence.* Think about your e-tivities in relation to your wider community, your discipline, your department and your latest research. What is really important in these areas? Use the key issue as a spark. Adapt your e-tivities as new theories and ideas arise.
- *Strategic intelligence.* Scan the literature for what's coming up and what might be important in the future, and use these ideas as goals and purposes for e-tivities. Create and convey vision and forward thinking in your participants.
- *Academic intelligence.* Put high value on the scholarship of ideas that arise out of your e-tivities and achievements, especially group outcomes. Recognize and celebrate effective learning that emerges. Especially highlight true engagement with a topic and with the construction of knowledge. Encourage the sharing of academic insights.
- *Reflective intelligence.* Build continually on the core skills and processes of monitoring, reflecting upon and evaluating every e-tivity. Look for knowledge that can be shared and built upon further.
- *Pedagogical intelligence.* You will have realized by now that developing expertise in online pedagogy is what e-tivities are all about. Pedagogical intelligence

refers to the complex and dynamic relationship between teaching and learning and is a key issue in the quality of e-tivities, ensuring that they are 'fit for purpose'. They need to be tried out, evaluated and constantly adjusted for this form of intelligence to flourish.

- *Collegial intelligence.* Recognize that e-moderators are learners too. Work together to improve good practice in your e-tivities. Share ideas within disciplines and across them. Work together online to increase your confidence and comfort with e-moderating, developing e-tivities and with virtual groups.

- *Emotional intelligence.* Allow the feelings of everyone involved in e-tivities to be surfaced, owned, expressed and respected. This is especially important with computer-mediated learning, where the technology itself may generate a wide range of positive and negative feelings. Try to foster opportunities for promoting interpersonal intelligence in your e-tivities through encouraging participants to appreciate a wide variety of points of view. Encourage intrapersonal intelligence through forming and developing models of understanding. There's more about emotional intelligence in Resources for Practitioners 11.

- *Spiritual intelligence.* Spiritual intelligence means tapping into the lives and development of each participant in an e-tivity in a way that will not necessarily be very tangible or measurable. This is the 'X' factor in e-tivities – a compassion that can be conveyed through online text. Create space to reflect on big issues. Watch out for their happening by chance – and foster any that you can!

- *Ethical intelligence.* Recognize and value the rights of all participants in e-tivities and foster the surfacing of the beliefs and values that underlie the online processes. Promote equality of access to the e-tivity opportunities that open up through technological access and motivation. E-moderate for equality and learning opportunities.

Time

Resources for practitioners 13:
Changing times

To benefit from new knowledge and to enjoy taking part in an online course, as a participant or an e-moderator, you need to find time. I asked some experienced, successful and happy e-moderators what they had given up when they started working online. At first they answered 'sleep' and 'TV'. After reflection, most said that they had not given anything up (much), but their lives had become more integrated and their use of time rather different from before.

> This is sad. The end is nigh! At times, I have had to steel myself to sit wearily at my computer, turning my back on family and other fairly pressing work to participate in this, initially strange, conference! :-). It hasn't been easy. It hasn't all been fun (for me). But it has been rewarding and a great experience that I have benefited from. I am now aware of another medium of instruction, of methods for promoting participation, of teaching, of facilitating, learning. . . I have entered the 24-hour society, at last. There's no going back. RC

Here are some ideas to help:

- Logging onto asynchronous courses in a regular rhythm – perhaps half an hour to an hour a day seems most productive for most people and it is likely to be most conducive to reflection and the least intrusive to life in general. By developing a regular routine, you won't let the number of messages mount to a level that will cause you undue work when you log on.
- Those with access from home and work, and maybe whilst travelling, seem to make the fastest adjustments.
- It's important to let colleagues at work, and/or family, know that when you're reading and typing on screen you are working and learning. Perhaps a little flag on the computer?
- Work with another person online to share time. (We have found that one e-moderator in Australia and one in Europe, or one in the United States and one in Asia, works well in handling time!)
- E-moderators should 'model' summarizing and archiving at stages 1–3 and after that encourage participants to take it in turns to summarize.

Resources for practitioners 14: The rhythm of online learning

> ## Dancing to the online music of time
>
> I have the pleasure of doing this course in work time, but it's easy to get distracted by the everyday tasks. My advice is to log on as often as possible (ideally at least once a day), even if it is only for a short time. SC

To handle time for participants, the habit of coming back regularly online and taking part is important. We call this a sense of 'rhythm'. Simple ideas go a long way.

- establish a pattern of online behaviour;
- model good online behaviour;
- be a builder;
- start small;
- start on time;
- get people to start together and move on together;
- give them a reason for being online;
- help them to develop a habit of coming back;
- large numbers of small e-tivities work better than one or two daunting ones;
- the e-moderator sets the environment and tone – make it welcoming;
- small interventions go a long way in providing support;
- encourage people to talk rather than giving them the answers;
- occasional quizzes and opportunities for personal feedback to participants from the e-moderator, however small, will help with pacing and rhythm.

Resources for practitioners 15: Time estimates

By far the commonest, and maybe the most important, question anyone ever asks me is 'How much time will preparing and running e-tivities take?' My estimates are given opposite.

Table II.2

---

1. *Staff time*
    1.1 E-moderators
    - 1.1.1 Think out the e-tivity, explore it with others and plan it well in advance. Estimate: 3 hours for the first time, 1 hour second and subsequent times.
    - 1.1.2 If you plan to issue resources that are copyrighted, leave time to get permission. Avoid this if you can.
    - 1.1.3 Write, quality-check and put invitation messages in place online. Estimate: 2 hours first time, 1 hour second and subsequent times. Pilot by asking others to read instructions and respond. 1 hour.
    - 1.1.4 Set up the bulletin board and resources. 1 hour first time, 0.5 hour after that.
    - 1.1.5 Respond to any e-mails and questions from participants or groups. 0.5 hour.
    - 1.1.6 Brief any team leaders if necessary. 0.5 hour.
    - 1.1.7 E-moderate the e-tivity. 2–3 hours per week.
    - 1.1.8 Summarize and plenarize. Extra 1–2 hours to close off.
    - 1.1.9 Evaluation and feed-forward to next time. 1 hour.

    1.2 Technical support
    - 1.1.10 Depends on platform and e-moderator's experience but may need 1–2 hours per e-tivity, especially at 1.1.3 and 1.1.4 and for the first time.
    - 1.1.11 Provide technical support and help to participants as necessary. 2 hours if participants are inexperienced, much less at stages 3–5.

2. *Participant time*
    - 2.1 Read invitation message, discuss online with other participants or e-moderator if necessary. 0.75 hour.
    - 2.2 Take part. 2–3 hours per week, more if fully collaborative.
    - 2.3 Explore, reflect, apply ideas, knowledge and understanding. 2 hours per week.
    - 2.4 Read and use summary. 1–2 hours.

Note:

Very discursive e-tivities such as those sometimes used in social sciences or humanities courses may need longer for e-moderators and e-tivities. Slow bulletin boards and forums may add to operational times.

Resources for practitioners 16: Planning e-tivity time

Plan Invitation

E-moderator posts instructions on. . .	[date]
Final plenary/summary message on. . .	[date]
Total number of days for e-tivity	[number]

Time commitment – in minutes

Minutes	E-moderator		Participant	
	Online	Offline	Online	Offline
Pre e-tivity actions, eg read, research (keep to absolute minimum)				
Actions during e-tivity				
Follow-up or post e-tivity actions				

General principle

At the lower levels of the five stages, participants need less time, e-moderators more. Further up the five-stage model, participants need more time, e-moderators less (except for summaries).

Resources for practitioners 17: E-moderators' time

What follows are some cause and effect ideas associated with developing and running e-tivities that have the most impact on the e-moderator's time. I suggest you use this page as a checklist and discussion document. Generally, more experience, training and support will reduce the time needed; less of them will increase it. However, note that the more successful you are at achieving good participation in e-tivities, the more the response and summarizing time from the e-moderator will rise. Our own little catch-22!

Also note that often at stages 1–3 of the five-stage model, e-moderators do more, participants less. At stages 4 and 5 students do more, e-moderators do less (but more carefully).

I present each of these issues in terms of quantities. You should be able to see how you can reduce or increase the amount of time by manipulating them.

E-moderator issues

- Amount and effectiveness of e-moderator's training.
- E-moderator's flexibility and organizational skills.
- E-moderator's skills and experience in weaving and summarizing.
- E-moderator's cultural background and language skills.
- The amount of other pressures on the e-moderator's time.
- The amount of the e-moderator's skill and experience in handling new constructs of online time.

The e-tivities

- Effectiveness and interest in the e-tivities by the participants.
- Participants' and e-moderator's emotional comfort with the online learning process.
- Amount of planning and resources that can be re-used.

Technical aspects

- Everyone's experience with the platform in use.
- Quality and appropriateness of systems and platform in use for the e-tivities.
- Levels and availability of good technical support.
- Whether the technology is easily available at any time and from any place.

Impact of success

The more successful you are, the more time you will spend online. The key variables are:

- the numbers of participants;
- the levels of contribution expected and achieved;
- levels of commitment and motivation from students, more contributions, more e-moderator time to respond and summarize;
- amount of browsing and vicarious learning. If more active participation is expected, e-moderators can spent huge amounts of time trying to persuade some participants to contribute.

Resources for practitioners 18: Counting the time

When designing your e-tivities it's clearly important to have a sense of how long both participants and e-moderators will need. Here are some tables to consider. The times that they give exclude designing and preparing the e-tivity and concentrate on the online time required from the moment that the first participant reads and responds to the e-tivity invitation.

These estimates are based on trained and experienced e-moderators and relatively straightforward messages. Novice e-moderators will take longer to read and summarize, untrained e-moderators will take very much longer. They may find the time commitment impossible. The length and complexity of messages also make a difference. For example, simpler and/or shorter messages can be expected from first-year undergraduates, compared with academics in a staff development programme.

Example 1

This is a simple e-tivity at stage 1 or 2 with a group of 15 participants. The e-tivity requires participants to put in some information already known to them, and to respond to messages from others. These timings assume an efficient forum platform that is easy to navigate around and easy to post messages to. Seconds spent waiting for a message to open or post can double these times.

Participants

Table II.3

Online action	No of messages to read	No of minutes spent reading	No of minutes spent writing/ posting
E-tivity 1: read and think	1	4	
Post message in response to e-tivity invitation			8
On a later visit, read contributions of 15 others	15	15	
Post response to the contributions of others (respond to two other messages)			8
Totals	16 messages	19 minutes	16 minutes

E-moderator

This e-moderator is fortunate that there is a quick summarizing function in her software platform to save time.

Table II.4

Online action	No of messages to read	No of minutes spent reading	No of minutes spent posting, archiving, summarizing and acknowledging
E-tivity 1, 15 initial postings plus 30 responses	45	45	
Quickly acknow-ledge each parti-cipant's initial response			15
Acknowledging further responses and summarizing			30
Totals	45	45	45

As you can see, for the simplest of e-tivities, the participant will spend 35 minutes directly engaged in the e-tivity, spread over at least two visits. And for the e-moderator, the commitment is 90 minutes, probably in at least three visits.

Example 2

This e-tivity is at level 3 and involves a slightly more complicated process of three groups of five investigating a topic, followed by a group plenary with all 15 participants involved.

Participants

Table II.5

Online action	No of messages to read	No of minutes spent reading	No of minutes spent writing/ posting
E-tivity 2, week 1: read e-tivity invitation and think	1	4	
Form into small groups, introductions and establish ways of working together	10	10	12
Undertake e-tivity in small groups, post output from small group into larger group plenary forum	20	20	30
Week 2, reform in larger groups. Read summaries from small groups	3	9	
Whole groups discussion, compare and contrast	30	30	15
Read e-moderator summary and critique	1	15	
Totals	65 messages	88 minutes	57 minutes

E-moderator

Table II.6

Online action	No of messages to read	No of minutes spent reading	No of minutes spent writing/ posting
E-tivity 2, week 1: answer questions about process and requirements	10	10	10
Briefly look into small groups to ensure all are working	10	10	
Remind of posting times into whole group plenary, and negotiate any extensions	5	5	20
Week 2, re-form in larger groups. Read summaries from small groups	3	9	
Whole groups discussion, compare and contrast, occasionally post to keep on track	20	20	10
Summarize plenary discussion and post closing message	30	30	30
Totals	78 (some revisited to undertake summary)	84	70

For this e-tivity, the participants have spent roughly half of their time (88 minutes) reading messages and a little less posting their own. Much of the e-moderator's time is concentrated at the end of week 2, in reading and providing a good summary and evaluation of the final plenary.

After stage 3, you can expect more reading and contributing time from participants, and more time for summarizing from e-moderators.

Resources for practitioners 19: Patterns of participation

Each individual participant develops his or her own pattern of logging on and taking part in a series of e-tivities. Opposite are the commonest patterns and some idea of how the e-moderator can help them.

Table II.7

Type	Behaviours	E-moderator response
The wolf	Visits once a week, lots of activity then disappears again until next week, or even the week after!	Nudge wolf by e-mail to encourage to visit again and see responses that s/he has sparked off.
The elephant	Steady – visits most days for a short time	Congratulate. Ask elephant to encourage and support others – especially mouse and squirrel.
The squirrel	Always catching up: completes two weeks in one session then disappears again for some time	Nudge squirrel by e-mail to suggest life is easier with more regular access. Check on other commitments. Provide regular summaries and archiving to enable squirrel to catch up easily and contribute.
The mouse	Visits once a week, reads and contributes little	Check that mouse can access all messages. Check language difficulties. May need boost of confidence. Give specific role
The mole	Inclined to post disembodied comments in a random way	Try to include relevant comments from mole in summaries and invite responses. Needs support and e-stroking.
The rabbit	Lives online, prolific message writer, responds very rapidly	Rabbit may need counselling to hold back and let others shine through. Give structured roles such as summarizing after a plenary.
The stag	Tendency to dominate discussion at certain times	Invite stag back frequently. Offer a structured and specific role.
The magpie	Steals ideas without acknowledging	Foster a spirit of acknowledgement and reinforcement of individual ideas. Warn magpie directly if necessary.
The dolphin	Intelligent, good communicator and playful online	Ensure dolphin acknowledges and works well with others. May annoy participants who think it's all very serious.

Online communication

Resources for practitioners 20: Learning 'Netspeak'

Talking online, sometimes called 'Netspeak', lacks the facial expressions, gestures and conventions that are important in communicating face to face and in conveying personal opinions and attitudes. In virtual worlds, participants and e-moderators alike must always be alert to the potential for ambiguity. This phenomenon has led to the development of 'smileys' or 'emoticons' as a substitute. Incidentally, the word 'emoticon' is derived from the term 'emote', which is used in virtual environments such as MUDs as a means to indicate a virtual *action* (Crystal, 2001).

There is little point in simply telling e-moderators and participants about Netspeak. Design a little e-tivity so they can understand and practise! Here are some ideas to try. E-tivities around these ideas are ideal for stages 1 and 2.

- *Netspeak* uses < > to indicate an *action,* such as a giggle or a look. Get everyone to show an action in their own networds. Abbreviations for action are fine if everyone understands them; for example, <g> for grin. It would be a good idea to explain new networds at least for the first two or three times you use them.
- *Capitals* are considered shouting. Invent other means of emphasis and see if they help with meaning.
- *Brevity* is all-important, mainly because of the length of time it takes both to type and then to read text on a screen. Try putting up sentences of different lengths and encouraging discussion on their effect.

- *Relevance.* Contributions should clearly relate to the purpose of the exchange. Always define purposes and constantly remind people about them. Be prepared to set up new areas for discussion if fresh issues come up, but make their purpose clear too.
- *Me too.* Much electronic communication is about people making their mark rather than adding a contribution as such. Set up an e-tivity to enable them to announce their arrival. Look for features in the software that help with saying 'me too'.

E-tivities to explore Netspeak

These e-tivities are suitable for stages 1 and 2. Participants generally enjoy them and they help introduce fluency in Netspeak:

- What would Moses say to the Israelites by e-mail or Web-based bulletin board?
- How would Kennedy's 'Berliner' speech come out online?
- Send an e-mail from one of the occupants of the *Mayflower*, halfway across the Atlantic.
- What did Caesar e-mail to the Britons before he invaded?
- Think up the best phrases for offering the following through e-mail: criticism, praise, challenge, support, sympathy. What are the differences compared to face to face?
- Can you paint a picture in words online to describe a fantastic sunset in your country?
- Can you describe the sounds outside your window at dawn?
- Start off a sentence. . . each participant finishes it.
- Play 'online' consequences. X met Y at Z (Web site). . . the consequence was. . .
- Try investigating Derek Rowntree's exploration of 'other voices are beginning to be heard' in distance education (http://www-iet.open.ac.uk/pp/D.G.F.Rowntree/words_in_de.htm – Rowntree, 1999) or Web site on words.

I find the Internet fascinating, it's such a source of information, isn't it? It can cover every aspect of our lives. You can find a range of jargon generators to really make you feel that your life is complete; for example, there's the Educational Jargon Generator at www.sciencegeek.net/lingo.html or the Postmodernism Generator if you want a whole essay to impress someone (http://www.elsewhere.org/cgi-bin/postmodern) and then there's the press-release generator when you want to really make a hit (http://www.nwfusion.com/buzz2000/pr.jsp). What other aspects of life can you find generators for? If you could invent an online phrase generator what would it do? JH

Resources for practitioners 21: Online language

Here are some suggestions to stimulate your thinking about the language we use or that we might use to describe interaction in the online world. They can also be used as e-tivity sparks at stage 2. Exploring these ideas helps people to realize that something very different and special is going on online. New labels may emerge as you try these terms out, or you might invent your own.

I've used the term 'Netspeak' in this book for the kind of action-based communications I've tried to harness. This term comes from David Crystal's excellent book about new types of language (Crystal, 2001). Some other terms are:

- Web speak: seems a little narrower. However, if you use Web speak, you need to remember that 'speak' means text, not voice.
- Weblish or Netlish. Some people prefer this term, which suggests a wider language and a cultural base. Maybe it does have a strong base in English but many people think that the Web will become increasingly multilingual.
- Cyberspeak: I think this one has perhaps been overused. I quite like it, though, because it suggests that there is another country called 'Cyber' – but is there?
- Electronic discourse: the more serious amongst you might like this one. It's straightforward and it is clearly about interchanges between people.
- Interactive written discourse: just a bit too long. But it's good in that it implies written and interactive, don't you agree?
- Neologisms. How do you feel about using made-up, action-based words (rather than longer, everyday phrases) such as e-tivities, e-moderating?

Resources for practitioners 22: Protocol

Most people are now familiar with online communication. However, it's worth exploring and reinforcing good styles and approaches, especially for e-tivities, where the action centres so much on text-based messaging. Good online communication cannot simply be directed or taught. Simply posting codes of practice or protocols on Web sites doesn't really achieve much, since guidelines need to be grounded and applied to be meaningful (McAteer *et al*, 2002).

You can use these lists as 'sparks' in e-tivities, and ask participants to apply them, work on them and, especially, build on them or invent their own. You might also like to encourage discussion on whether, if you make 'rules', they can easily be applied.

Using electronic communication

Message conventions

Use e-mail to message one or several specific people, or to address messages directly to people who need to take action or who need to reply to you and to copy the messages for information to people who you believe need to know about the content – but think first before sending an unnecessary message!

Use group conferencing, bulletin board or forum when the message is intended for everyone in a particular group, such as in response to an e-tivity and when you expect that everyone will have the right to reply.

- Never copy on a message to anyone not on the original list, nor into a group area, without asking and receiving the permission of the originator of the message.

- If you reply to just one part of someone else's message, copy and paste their words into the start of your e-mail, so it's clear which sections you are referring to.
- Choose a short, effective, enticing title for your message.
- If you reply to someone and change the subject, change the title too.
- Be prepared to describe how you feel as well as what you think.
- Avoid putting words into capital letters – they are considered to be equivalent to shouting.
- Ensure that you place new messages in the *appropriate* place.
- Keep to one topic per message with a relevant title. It's far better to send several short message with different titles than one long one covering many subjects.
- If you need to make a number of points in a message, label them 1, 2, 3. . . This way it is easy to reply.
- You can build 'groups' of people to e-mail for your convenience. Use these cautiously and only when your message concerns everyone in that group. Using a forum might be better.
- If you receive an e-mail message that has been addressed to a number of people, think carefully before replying to all of them. You might only need to make the comment to the originator of the message, or one or two other people. Some people get *very annoyed* about many minor e-mails circulating around large groups.
- If you receive a message that contains a 'reply all' to a large group including you, and which you consider irrelevant, simply delete it. Treat it as junk mail. Avoid replying to 'all' again in your anger and perpetuating the problem.
- Avoid setting up automatic replies to messages if you are away, unless really necessary. Try instead to pick them up from wherever you are.

Attaching documents to message

- Make sure the title is clear and there are one or two lines of description in the message so that your recipients can decide whether, and how soon, they need to download the document.
- Be sure that your recipients have suitable software to download and open your document.
- Always check a document for viruses, using up-to-date virus checking software, before you send it to others.

Participants

Resources for practitioners 23: Contributions

You might find my nine categories for analysing contributions to e-tivities helpful, especially at stage 4. They work best in discussion-type forums or where there is an online plenary following an e-tivity. The analytical categories make it easier to see what is happening in the debate.

If you wish to assess for contribution, they provide a framework.

Table II.8

	Individual thinking
1	Offering up ideas or resources and inviting a critique of them
2	Asking challenging questions
3	Articulating, explaining and supporting positions on issues
4	Exploring and supporting issues by adding explanations and examples
5	Reflecting on and re-evaluating personal opinions
	Interactive thinking
6	Offering a critique, challenging, discussing and expanding ideas of others
7	Negotiating interpretations, definitions and meanings
8	Summarizing and modelling previous contributions
9	Proposing actions based on ideas that have been developed

Resources for practitioners 24: Avoiding stereotypes and prejudicial actions

Ensuring fairness and equality in online groups is a challenge for *everyone* involved (Hodgson, 2002). It's possible to 'get it wrong' and stand in the way of active contributions and positive feelings. One way to start is to explore the way prejudice affects written and interactive communication.

Prejudices are a kind of emotional learning that occurs early in our lives. They are hard to eradicate, even in adults who feel they should not be prejudiced. The power of stereotypes in our minds is that they are largely self-confirming. We remember incidents that confirm our prejudices and forget those that discount them. This makes it hard to recognize prejudice in ourselves and to convince groups of the damage caused by them to productive learning.

So as an e-moderator, it is important to know that you will have some deep-rooted and possibly subtly working prejudices yourself, and so will everyone else in the group. It's unlikely that in the time you are working with the group you can seriously change this. What you can do, though, is to ensure that online behaviours – what people do and say – do not reinforce or act upon those feelings.

Online, there are two particular issues that make it more likely that individuals will feel offended.

First, everything that is 'said' is available for viewing and reviewing by everyone. Participants can therefore read many times something that might have offended. They may feel that they must respond because other people will otherwise have their prejudices reinforced.

Second, there is a lack of tone and body language in 'Netspeak'. Sometimes intention and meaning are conveyed less accurately than in face-to-face encounters by inexperienced participants.

These problems are relatively uncommon. Most online participants are careful, reflective and supportive of each other. However, we must never turn a blind eye and ignore any act of potential discrimination in our groups, because the learning of individuals and of the whole group may suffer. This sometimes means taking a stance against something that might be considered trivial and unimportant to many people – a sexist joke for instance.

Humour also needs to be used with care. The wider the cultural mix or the scaling up of your e-tivities, the more likely it is that one participant will offend another. What is considered humour is very diverse. It's the e-moderator's role to spot and respond quickly to such issues. However, if the group is well established, then others will help too. As an example, the following is an actual sequence that took place recently in a trainee e-moderators' course. All names have been changed.

20 November
From: Marion Martin (participant)

> If I am feeling a bit down I sometimes have a look at www.uglypeople.com as it makes me laugh! I would use the ugly people Web site to encourage students to post something – at stage 2 for socializing.

21 November
From: Daniel Sanders (e-moderator)

> Hi Marion, thanks for this opportunity to disagree on a subject that might be sensitive for some participants. Since we don't know what any of our participants look like (unless they have sent a picture) and looks are rather subjective anyway, there may be a danger of some of us feeling that we look like one of the people featured on the site. This might generate feelings that may be hard for some to express online, thus putting some in a position where they are uncertain how to respond.
>
> In working with your students, I suggest that any sensitive topics are left until the group feels comfortable enough to challenge each other's contributions.
>
> What do others think? Daniel

21 November
From: Cecily Smith (participant)

> Marion, I concur with Daniel's words of caution! We have no idea whether our course participants have physical disabilities or irregularities that they have been teased about. On the other hand, given my sense of humour, I actually found the site a bit of a laugh. I guess that humour is something that is shared between people who know each other fairly well and therefore has the potential to backfire, especially online.
>
> Whenever I quote sites to people I try to give them a short précis about what the site contains. Then they can decide whether they actually want to visit it. Mind you, I am sure you are thinking that Ugly.com is pretty self-explanatory. Cheers Cecily

22 November
From: Hannah Sparm (participant)

> Daniel Sanders writes: 'I suggest that any sensitive topics are left until the group feels comfortable enough to challenge each other's contributions. What do others think?'
>
> I felt quite threatened when two of the participants from this group seemed to disagree with me in e-tivity 3.4, so I hesitate to reply to this as I don't want to upset Marion; however, I think the issue is important.
>
> I felt that the Web site is an unkind one. I have a very dear friend who has been suicidal. She feels that she is fat and that everyone despises her for it. She has a beautiful Ferrari but finds it difficult to get out of the car at petrol stations for the fear that people will think 'Nice car, shame about the driver.' From previous discussions we have had, I know that she would be mortified to see this Web site.
>
> I have learnt hugely from your thoughtful contributions to the e-tivities, Marion, so please forgive me when I say that I think that this is not a good avenue to pursue.
>
> With very best wishes, Hannah

23 November
From: Marion Martin (participant)

Many apologies to everyone who found the Web site not the most appropriate under e-moderating or any other circumstances. On reflection, it was poor judgement on my part.

Colleagues, you bring a valuable lesson in understanding the nature of this medium and I think all your points were valid. I found the nature and tone of your comments very supportive and it made me realize that humour is a very personal choice.

However, it has some positive outcomes:

- contributions have been challenged;
- a valuable lesson has been learnt (by me for the future);
- although I sit downhearted as I write this, supportive comments from the group have been gratefully received and acknowledged, which still make me feel as an accepted and valued member of the group.

Thanks, Marion

Resources for practitioners 25: Disabilities and e-tivities

Because of their simplicity, e-tivities offer online group learning to participants with disabilities that might hinder their capacity to take part in more conventional learning activities. In some countries, legislation requires at least minimum access to courseware for disabled learners. E-tivities help, as they are based largely on simple text-based messages and enable all contributions to be valued equally.

Online, disabilities and special needs are rarely obvious unless the participant chooses to write about them. People with speech or hearing difficulties are not at any disadvantage in text-based messaging.

Technology can help or hinder, of course. Keyboard or speech commands can be provided for those unable to use a mouse. Electronic text can be designed so that it converts to Braille. With forethought, Web pages can be designed to be more effective for certain disabilities, although the increased emphasis on graphics has created new challenges. In constructing e-tivities, consider the font and style and how they might look on a variety of screens and to different people. This will help those with partial visual impairment, but will also be of benefit to all participants.

Mobility

Learning online can be an open door for those with restricted mobility or difficulty in accessing buildings. E-tivities provide opportunities to 'travel', meet and learn with others with comparative ease, if accessible materials and processes are on offer.

Participants who have problems with their vision or physical movement might find that the keyboard and screen prevent them from contributing as much as they would like, or as quickly as others. For example, those who cannot freely move their hands and arms may not use the keyboard at a reasonable speed and need special equipment or speech recognition software. However, the short 'bursts' of activity required by e-tivities, and the emphasis on contribution rather than reading, often help with attention and mobility problems.

Dyslexia

Participants with learning difficulties, such as dyslexia, often find that they can contribute better through their keyboards and through asynchronous bulletin boards and forums, than they can in synchronous chat rooms, face-to-face meetings or paper-based writing. They have an opportunity to rearrange their words and sentences before committing them to the rest of the group. However, they will have more difficulty if the platform does not offer a spell checker for all their text. They can prepare messages in a word processor, spell-check and then upload, but this may slow their responses. Everyone, however, needs to be reassured that mistakes in typing or spelling are not important with e-tivities. It's the thought or contribution that counts! The odd spelling or grammatical error should worry nobody.

Vision

Blind participants cannot use a mouse so need to become adept at keyboard commands. They can adapt software through Braille printouts of messages or through using speech synthesis. An experienced intermediary is needed to train and support blind users to the point of competence and independence. When changes are made to the system, blind participants must be notified early so that they can arrange in advance for specific adaptations and training.

Blind users frequently develop good keyboard skills for inputting. In an emergency they can have short e-tivities read to them.

Resources for practitioners 26: Are you addicted to e-tivities?

The following questions are not meant too seriously, but they aim to promote self-reflection. You can use them as a light e-tivity at stage 1 or for a fun review at the end of a programme. Ask participants to suggest others:

- Do you wake up at 2 am to go to the bathroom and then can't resist logging on quickly just to see what's happening?
- Do you sign off and find that you were online for two hours without a break instead of the one hour you planned?
- Do you reply in Netspeak when someone speaks to you face to face?
- Is your first reaction to a question: 'I'll look it up on the Web'?
- Have you set aside a special room (shrine?) for your PC?
- Do you think of all of your friends by their screen names?
- Do others in the house complain that they can never get access to the PC?
- Do you believe that if something is not on the Net, then it's not worth knowing about?
- Do you completely deny that you are a two-computer family?
- Do you get excited about broadband?
- Do you know what GPS means?
- Does your horse/tree/cat have her own home page?
- Do you e-mail the person sitting opposite you in the office?
- Have you bought your grandmother a new mouse for her birthday?
- Have you considered the colour of your iMac when planning the colour scheme of your dining area?
- Do you get called to supper by text message?
- Have you cancelled your TV subscription?
- Have you tried downloading an interesting-looking pizza?
- Do you know what the term 'fruitless browsing' means?
- Are you a compulsive collector of Web site addresses?
- Do you feel that you have to build a database for your favourite URLs?
- Do you check out the Internet café before the fire escape in your holiday hotel?
- Do you listen to the radio when you use your computer?
- Do you pack your computer for your holiday before your swimsuit?
- Do you get excited about the Internet café in your holiday resort?
- Are you willing to queue for Internet access?
- Do you check e-mails before turning on the coffee pot in the morning?

E-moderating

Resources for practitioners 27: Recruiting e-moderators

Example interview questions

These questions can be used in a face-to-face interview, but can also work just as well as an online interview – conducted, for example, through e-mail.

Table II.9

Quality/ characteristic	1. CONFIDENT	2. CONSTRUCTIVE
Understanding of online process A	1. What experience do you have as an online learner? 2. In what ways has working online changed your thinking? 3. What do you think are the critical success factors for online learning?	13. Give examples of typical messages on screen, ask for reactions/responses. 14. Describe your favourite teaching or learning experience.
Technical skills B	4. Have you used ★★★ software? What do you need to be confident in its use? 5. How did you acquire your keyboard skills?	15. What one development of the Web and Internet do you think will most affect the success of online learning?

Table II.9 *(continued)*

Quality/ characteristic	1. CONFIDENT	2. CONSTRUCTIVE
	6. Have you any experience of reading on screen, eg marking and commenting on assignments? 7. Have you access to the Internet from 1) home, 2) office, 3) when travelling?	
Online communication skills C	8. Send us an example (with identities removed) of what you would consider good e-mail and bad e-mail? 9. What is the best tip you have for saving time when working online?	16. Give an actual example of a message you have sent to soothe an online emotion 17. Give examples of how you would respond to . . . *(provide participants' messages).*
Content expertise D	10. What is your favourite Web site at the moment? Give the URL. How could you use it as an e-tivity 'spark'?	18. What are the best online resources for your discipline? How can they be productively incorporated into online interaction? 19. Show us an example of a summary of an online discussion and suggest its strengths and weaknesses.
Personal characteristics E	11. What books/papers have you read about e-moderating/online teaching or training? 12. What kind of training or support do you need to be successful as an online teacher?	20. In what ways can you establish your identity on a conference, with a group of people you may never meet?

Resources for practitioners 28: E-moderator competencies

Table II.10 *E-moderator competencies*

Quality/ characteristic	RECRUIT		TRAIN		DEVELOP	
	1. CONFIDENT	2. CONSTRUCTIVE	3. DEVELOPMENTAL	4. FACILITATING	5. KNOWLEDGE SHARING	6. CREATIVE
Understanding of online process A	Personal experience as an online learner, flexibility in approaches to teaching and learning. Empathy with the challenges of becoming an online learner	Able to build online trust and purpose for others. Understand the potential of online learning and groups	Ability to develop and enable others, act as catalyst, foster discussion, summarize, restate, challenge, monitor understanding and misunderstanding, take feedback	Know when to control groups, when to let go, how to bring in non-participants, know how to pace discussion and use time online, understand the five-stage scaffolding process and how to use it	Able to explore ideas, develop arguments, promote valuable threads, close off unproductive threads, choose when to archive	Able to use a range of approaches from structured activities (e-tivities) to freewheeling discussions, and to evaluate and judge success of these
Technical skills B	Operational understanding of software in use, reasonable keyboard skills, able to read fairly comfortably on screen, good, regular, mobile access to the Internet	Able to appreciate the basic structures of online conferencing, and the Web and Internet's potential for learning	Know how to use special features of software for e-moderators, eg controlling, weaving, archiving. Know how to 'scale up' without consuming inordinate amounts of personal time, by using the software productively	Able to use special features of software to explore learner's use, eg message history, summarizing, archiving	Able to create links between other features of learning programmes, introduce and e-tivities and to online resources without diverting participants from interaction	Able to use software facilities to create and manipulate conferences and to generate an online learning environment, able to use alternative software and platforms
Online communication skills C	Courteous and respectful in online (written) communication, able to pace and use time appropriately	Able to write concise, energizing, personable online messages	Able to engage with people online (not the machine or the software), respond to messages appropriately, be appropriately 'visible' online, elicit and manage students' expectations	Able to interact through e-mail and conferencing, and achieve interaction between others, be a role model. Able to gradually increase the number of participants dealt with successfully	Able to value diversity with cultural sensitivity; explore differences and meanings	Able to communicate comfortably without visual cues, able to diagnose and solve problems and opportunities online, use humour online, use and work with

					online, without huge amounts of extra personal time	emotion online, handle conflict constructively
Content expertise D	Knowledge and experience to share, willingness to add own contributions	Able to encourage sound contributions from others, know of useful online resources for their topic	Able to trigger debates by posing intriguing questions. Know when to intervene, when to hold back	Know about valuable resources (eg on the Web) and use them as sparks in e-tivities	Carry authority by awarding marks fairly to students for their participation, contributions and learning outcomes	Able to enliven conferences through use of multi-media and electronic resources, able to give creative feedback and build on participants' ideas
Personal characteristics E	Determination and motivation to become an e-moderator	Able to establish an online identity as e-moderator	Able to adapt to new teaching contexts, methods, audiences and roles	Know how to create *and sustain* a useful, relevant online learning community	Show a positive attitude, commitment and enthusiasm for online learning	

Resources for practitioners 29: Contingent e-moderating

It is almost impossible to predict in advance which participants will need help to actively learn online and who will sail through the e-tivities with joy. Some participants need a lot of help, but do not recognize this, or do not wish to ask for it. Contingent e-moderating is a solution. These ideas might also be helpful to IT people.

I have borrowed heavily from the concepts of Wood and Wood (1999) on contingent tutoring. Their model is based on good face-to-face interactions.

The principles are easy to state, though a little harder to achieve in online practice. However, it's really worthwhile trying, as participation and contribution rates shoot up, and wasted time is reduced.

- If a participant seems to be in trouble (spotted either by non-contribution or cries for help), an e-moderator should offer immediate help, or direct the participant to a source of help (especially if the problem is technical).
- The e-moderator should focus very closely on what *task* the participant is trying to achieve. Try to prevent anyone going down a pathway of blame, anger and wanting immediately to give up. Try to keep everyone calm and focused on achieving the task required. Don't become diverted.
- The e-moderator should ask the participants a few pointed questions about exactly what they are trying to achieve and what they perceive the problem to be before offering help. Try also to establish what they know already. Then offer a way forward.
- If this does not solve the problem then very much more explicit instructions should be given, perhaps through another medium of communication. It may even be necessary to get someone to sit with the participant and go through what to do – to bring in local face-to-face help.
- No 'dependency' should be set up, however, and as soon as the participant shows signs of taking part, he or she should be directed back into the group e-tivities. The participant may need a little more 'acknowledging' and praising than average for a while.

Resources for practitioners 30: Running e-tivity plenaries

Weaving, archiving and summarizing are key tasks for e-moderators and add much value to e-tivities. Participants can also usefully acquire and contribute these skills. Or the role of summarizer can be taken by two or three people working collaboratively (however, this takes up more time). Whoever undertakes the summary should always invite comment, by the original contributors, on its sufficiency and interpretation.

Weaving

Here is an example of clever 'weaving' of contributions, using quotes from six different messages during an online discussion about the e-moderator's role and dominant and lurking participants. The summarizer and weaver is JS and his contributions are in italics.

> 'D said, "We need to be in the conference regularly as a lot of damage can be done if you weren't there at the 'bud-nipping' stage".
>
> *I'd go along with that one but bearing in mind A's point that* "There do have to be parameters otherwise those who can only spend minimum time feel disadvantaged by others who become addicts!" *and a moderator should not need to become an addict to do the job well.*
>
> 'So, I think I'll be more assertive this time round' *(A's message).*

'*Yes, be assertive (when appropriate !) even if . . .*'

'the flaming has broken out, not between the combatants, but against the poor old e-moderator when he or she has intervened to break it up!' *(H's message)*.

'. . . *not looking forward to that one coming my way. Hopefully, however, we will generally be in a position to* "let students get on with discussions if these seem productive." ' *(P's message)*

'. . . *and as C says,* "it actually sounds fun".'

JS

Summarizing

The purpose of summarizing is:

- To weave and acknowledge the variety of ideas and contributions.
- To refocus discussion and activity when postings are too numerous. Summarize after each 20 messages, at a pre-agreed time or at regular intervals, for example every three days. In a large or busy e-tivity, this can be done daily.
- To refocus discussion and activity when postings have strayed from the topic.
- To refocus discussion and promote activity when e-tivities are going well.
- To refocus discussion and revive activity when postings are flagging.
- To signal closure of the e-tivity.
- To take the outcomes of an e-tivity to present or work on offline.
- To provide fresh starting points for broadening and deepening discussion.
- To remind participants of the journey they have travelled.
- To reinforce and 'imprint' new information and knowledge.
- To provide a 'spark' for a new e-tivity.
- To provide a 'footprint' as a spark for a new group.

Archiving

Archiving means removing messages to a different place in the online platform, preferably still easily retrievable by participants. Archives help enormously to prevent e-tivity message boards and conferences becoming overwhelming, particularly for newcomers and at stages 1 and 2. The e-moderator should indicate to participants how to find and look at the archived discussions, if they wish to.

Archiving is excellent as a way of filing away sets of discussions for later use or as reference or research material, for others who want to revisit the discussions. When you archive, it's ethical to make it clear how messages may later be used, and seek permission of the contributors.

Archive:

- To facilitate storage and retrieval.
- When postings are too numerous to handle effectively.
- If there are many participants coming in, or some coming in late.
- When the discussion activity is concluded and participants have a satisfactory summary.
- To facilitate comparison between discussion themes.

Resources for practitioners 31: Unexpected outcomes

Here are some examples of unexpected outcomes to e-tivities. You might like to consider how you would handle, or avoid, these situations.

Message 1

The amount of money spent online in Australia is only about 1 per cent of the amount of money spent in shops. I posted this fact to my students and asked them to discuss it. They spent all their time talking about what personally they had or had not bought online, which was not what I expected. Sharon

Message 2

Most of my students are interested in football. We had a fantasy football e-tivity. It started off as a good-natured affair with people chatting about their teams. Then all of a sudden it went mad and very competitive and now there is a group of people who spend their time abusing everyone and anyone, including their colleagues, and the culture is unpleasant. Paul

Message 3

The software was unwieldy and it was difficult to follow a thread through. It was not easy to follow the 'argument' from note to note. In the end, everyone started 'talking' about quite different things and three separate conversations started. Sally

Message 4

As the deadline for the finish of the e-tivity came close, everyone seemed to come online at once. One evening, seven out of the 12 people involved were online together and messages were popping up all over the place. Felicity

Message 5

We put up an e-tivity asking how people could support or offer to help others online. I thought they would talk about how to use counselling skills online but I was wrong. Some participants posted up the Web sites for their companies, others offered their personal e mails. Mary

Provision for e-tivities

Resources for practitioners 32: A recipe for e-learning

All seems too complicated for you? Try this!

Ingredients

- A good course of proven quality, presented by 'old' methods.
- An audience that wants this topic and new methods and has good regular Internet access.
- A few committed flexible people, with experience of teaching the course or the topic.

Recipe

- Start from where you are and what you do well.
- Decide what aspects of the course would benefit from the technology.
- Train one or two people as e-moderators.
- Consider the ways in which the course might be scalable.
- Check what e-learning applications are available to you at direct or low costs with really good technical support.
- Design the course and the Web site on the basis of low-cost and easy to run e-tivities.
- Provide the learners with a clear pacing structure.
- Pilot the course with not more than two groups.
- Evaluate by asking the learners.
- Continue to develop your e-moderators and train more.
- Share your ideas with others and learn from their response.
- Scale up the participant numbers by 100 per cent each time you deliver the course.

Resources for practitioners 33: E-tivities and costs

Once e-tivities are designed and built into a programme, the key issue is the cost of arranging appropriate e-moderator support. Therefore it is important to know as soon as possible how many participants are likely to arrive and when. Clearly, the amount, availability and skill of support from people other than the e-moderator, such as those providing technical help, or online social hosts and mentors, will strongly affect the efficiency of the e-moderator's time.

Here are some ways to keep down the costs of deploying e-tivities:

- Make clear decisions about roles and numbers of e-moderators that you will need and the participant : e-moderator ratio.
- Encourage e-moderators to work in small teams, covering for and supporting each other.
- Double the impact of trained and experienced e-moderators by encouraging them to e-moderate two or three groups of participants at any time.
- Keep your e-moderator support to participants focused and specify what you expect them to do and when – if necessary, publish the total number of hours per week or month available to participants.
- Establish early on how much e-moderators should expect to do, and what are reasonable expectations on the part of participants
- Ensure that e-moderators are trained in designing, developing and running efficient and effective e-tivities. Train e-moderators in advance of starting work with their participants.
- Train e-moderators online, rather than face to face.
- Train e-moderators using the online platform itself, thus creating confidence in the platform as well as creating an e-moderating skill base.
- Ensure that e-moderators can up- and download messages offline if they wish.
- Train e-moderators in how to use your software or platform software to best advantage to save time.
- Set up good helpdesk and online support systems, preferably available 24 hours, and encourage competent participants to support others, leaving more of your e-moderators' online time for learning-related e-moderating.
- Use existing resources and knowledge constructed online as much as possible rather than developing materials and/or paying for expensive third party materials.
- Develop systems for re-use, recycling and sharing of e-tivities invitational instruction messages.
- Build up economies of scale as rapidly as possible – choose only systems and approaches that can be expanded cheaply.

See Ash and Bacsich (2002) for more about costs of networked learning.

Resources for practitioners 34:
Find out about your platform

Individuals very rarely make choices of technology platforms for teaching and learning. Usually complex, highly politicized processes are involved and choices are part of wider strategic questions, implications and decisions. This resource offers some key questions for teaching staff to ask. I hope this resource will result in increased dialogue between stakeholders and more productive exploration of options and needs about learning technologies.

Online platforms are variously named virtual learning environments (VLEs), managed learning environments (MLEs) or learning management systems (LMSs). Sometimes they are called computer-mediated conferencing (CMC) environments, asynchronous learning networks (ALNs) or computer-supported learning (CSL).

Online platforms all work a little differently, look a little different and offer different characteristics. Most environments offer the development and presentation of Web pages as well as bulletin boards and forums. Some offer most of the functions that you might want for all kinds of online learning, such as synchronous and multi-media capabilities, or assessment tools, but some are more limited. Most include more functions than you really will need for designing and running e-tivities. The MLEs and the LMSs typically include a range of functions beyond teaching and learning, such as the registration of students, the recording of grading and assessments, and the transactions associated with student and financial information. Managed learning environments and LMSs also track and record the progress of the learners through their programmes.

Most organizations choose a commercially provided system, though some have 'home-grown' technology platforms. Off-the-shelf platforms rarely result in all stakeholders being satisfied with all of the functions and there are usually some problems with integration with other organizational systems. Bespoke online environments, such as those developed in-house, integrate more comfortably with existing practices and systems but are critically dependent on the continuing availability of the people who built them.

Most of the providers of platforms are quite small businesses and they frequently combine and regroup. Most of the technology platforms are still in their infancy. They lack the diversity and capabilities that come with the maturation of technologies. Currently there is no system or platform that has been adopted throughout all levels of education or countries. There is no one technology platform that suits every organization, discipline or programme. However, after a platform has been chosen, considerable investment goes into setting up the hardware and software, recruiting and training technical staff and solving problems. Therefore, platforms become 'embedded' in the way the teaching and learning organization goes about its business and they are difficult and expensive to change.

What you should know, however, is that it's possible to design and run e-tivities with either the most sophisticated or the simplest programme. The e-tivity approach will work in all of them.

Operational questions

If a platform is already in place, or chosen, here are questions for teaching and learning staff, in their role as e-moderators, to ask:

- Do not ask 'what can the platform do for me?' but 'what can I do with it?'
- Does this platform emphasize the delivery of learning resources, or interaction between participants? If both, what is the balance?
- What are its special affordances, characteristics and limitations?
- Can I learn to e-moderate online through the platform itself? (If not, why not?)
- How can I adapt the platform to suit my current and planned teaching and learning practices?
- How will this platform help me to creative active and interactive learning?
- How will e-tivities work in this platform? Can I create and change them easily quickly and independently?
- What special features does this platform offer to help promote group participation, deal with the emotional aspects of learning in groups and save and manage time?
- What provision does the platform make for participants with disabilities?
- Can I share an identity (eg 'e-moderator'), share resources and work in a team with colleagues? What features will help?

Training in the platform

Early adopters are usually happy to spend many hours engaging in exploration and experimentation with platforms for teaching. But when attempts are made to scale up the introduction of technology, many more teaching staff need to get involved. Demonstrations are usually carried out by the IT professionals or by enthusiasts. Often, quite naturally, the technical features of the platform are emphasized. If 'resistance' from teaching staff is noticed then additional 'hands-on' sessions are offered. Regrettably, this well-intentioned process has resulted in many thousands of teachers in many contexts believing that teaching and learning online is about computing and that it's difficult to grasp. Then a vicious circle results: they think, 'If I cannot easily see the benefits of online, what chance do my participants stand?'

Even if teachers have an excellent record in conventional settings it is difficult to predict whether they will do well as e-moderators. Currently, few universities and colleges offer much in the way of training for e-moderating skills and the best methods are yet to be identified (Kearsley, 2000). However, we do know that the acquisition of e-moderating skills cannot be achieved vicariously by, for example, lecturers observing other online teachers or by looking at exemplary Web sites.

Clearly, for staff development to be successful, training needs to be rooted in the peculiarities and requirements of the online environment itself. It needs to engage staff in the experience of working with others online and to be focused on the usefulness and relevance of online learning. In my view, by far the best way of introducing new technology is to ensure that teaching staff first experience the platform as participants and within their own communities of practice. Therefore, the first and key role for the online platform is that it is easy and successful to build a staff development programme in it, which engages and supports teachers on their journeys to becoming e-moderators.

Ask your platform provider:

- Can you help train me as an e-moderator or show me development programmes in the software itself? (If not, why not?)
- What special skills will I need to ensure my exploitation of and my independence in your platform?
- What investment in my time will be needed before I can successfully design, post and run e-tivities in this platform?
- How can I best prepare myself for the challenge of engaging with all participants equally on your platform? What special features does it offer to help me ensure equal opportunities?
- Who else has used e-tivities in your platform in my discipline and can you put me in touch?

Getting involved in choosing

There are some key functions that are important for the most successful design and development of e-tivities and for effective and efficient e-moderating.

- Are the discussions between participants and e-moderators automatically (or easily) recorded? If the answer is no to this question, it will be harder for the e-moderator to explore the success of his or her e-tivities, and continuously improve.
- In what form will the records be available to the e-moderators and how can they make sure that inappropriate others do not have access to them?
- Is it easy to capture a variety of views of interactions between the participants – for example, what the group did on a particular day, what an individual has achieved over one month, what the pattern of communication between the e-moderator and the group is?
- The platform needs to make scaffold building easy for the five-stage model. Therefore, the process of making links between e-tivity processes (rather than published resources) should be obvious. Is this the case? How exactly will this work? Will e-moderators be able to set up these links for themselves?
- It is also best if stimulating 'sparks' and discussion occur and be presented simply *on the same* Web page. Can the platform offer this?
- The platform can help by offering facilities that enable e-moderators to do what they need to do most of, more efficiently and effectively. These special features should include very easy *summarizing* of participants' messages, archiving and deleting. Ask for this to be demonstrated or built. If it is not available, e-moderators will spend much more time e-moderating the e-tivities, but less effectively.
- Does the platform include very easy ways of synchronous chat and 1 : 1 chat messages built into the asynchronous bulletin board? These are useful for bridging activities between the stages of the model.
- Will the platform be fast, whether through client or browser-based access to the software, and accessible from low-specification machines both at work and at home and when travelling? Slow bulletin boards reduce interaction between participants.
- Will the platform enable e-moderators to see who is online at any one time, easily determine the frequency of their visits and what they did when they were there? Will the e-moderator be able to access this information for him- or herself, without relying on technical support?
- Does the platform have a way of submitting assignments and assessment electronically? Does it include effective ways of offering quizzes and self-evaluation for individuals and groups? Does it include structured ways of giving fast feedback?

- How exactly will equal opportunities be addressed? How will participants with a range of disabilities be able to take part? Can we see the reference sites for these? (If not, why not?)
- Are you promising features that we want and are not currently available? What guarantees will you offer on these?

The Web site associated with this book (www.e-tivities.com) offers you a series of links to explore online learning platforms.

E-tivities background

Resources for practitioners 35: E-tivities roots: a bibliography

This resource runs through some of the main underlying concepts for e-tivities from which I have drawn my research, for those who would like to explore further. I hope this background will encourage you to see that many approaches to teaching and learning are still as relevant in the online world as they were before anyone mentioned the term 'Internet'.

As a 'spark' for this resource, I take the words of Jonathan Darby:

> The mule is a hybrid creature that can only be produced through the union of two different species, but from this union comes a vigour that exceeds that of either parent. Networked learning requires a similar union between the traditional strengths of higher education institutions and the entrepreneurship of the business sector. (Darby, 2002: 25)

Knowledge circulation

There are many different ideas about knowledge, supported by a large range of literature. For example, for Plato, knowledge comes from pure reason and logical thought, and it is the essence of being human. For Aristotle, knowledge comes from our senses. We know about the world and seek to understand it through empirical evidence (this is the basis of positivism and the scientific method).

Concepts for knowledge creation and sharing for e–tivities are drawn from ideas of knowledge as being constructed (Weick, 1995). We view 'knowing' as an active and personal process (Cook and Brown, 1999). Knowledge itself is of many kinds. Some types of knowledge come from knowing how, what, who, why. Other kinds we can acquire only through experience, such as playing a musical instrument or riding a bicycle. We can internalize this kind of actively acquired knowledge but cannot communicate it to others, as they have to practise or experience it for themselves. Some knowledge can be expressed (often called codified) in language (such as English, mathematics, Cobol), but this is only information that a recipient has to interpret to create meaning for him- or herself. Meaning is a process of sense making, relating it to existing known concepts in order to turn it into useful knowledge for an individual. For Polanyi (1962, 1966), all knowledge has a tacit dimension: not everything can be codified.

How do we acquire knowledge? We learn through interaction with others and, given half a chance, we quickly spread that knowledge, although in many groups there are appreciable barriers to knowledge sharing. The reason why people collaborate is associated with a *purpose*. When a group *needs* to work together for a *reason*, then more knowledge may be created through the interactions (McDermott, 1999).

Knowledge circulates through communities in many ways. Often we think of knowledge as being in books, articles and in people's minds – hence the importance given to the 'keynote' speech at terrestrial conferences, although if you accept my description in the previous paragraphs, then you will see this as really data and information being exchanged. A big literature on 'storytelling' has emerged recently as a way of sharing experiences and expressing tacit knowledge (Brown and Duguid, 2000; Churchill, Snowdon and Munro, 2001). For example, in management thinking, the telling of 'war stories' from the 'front line' to otherwise quite isolated senior managers has always been considered an important form of knowledge. In teaching, much practice is developed quite informally, from trial and error and from discussion in teachers' common rooms. Recently, my aspiring actor daughter told me that even in highly competitive audition situations, most candidates are extremely supportive, helping each other practise for parts or auditions and by exchanging information on good sources of materials and contacts. E-tivities attempt to tap into, structure and provide an ongoing supportive environment for this kind of information sharing and knowledge construction.

Constructivism and situated learning

Making learning personally meaningful comes from the constructivist perspect-ive, which emphasizes collaboration between peers and teachers within support-ive frameworks, in this case, the online learning environment (Duffy and Cunningham, 1996). Situated learning emphasizes learning happening in context and the importance of relevant and authentic tasks that can be applied to the participants' everyday learning, working and cognition (Fox, 2002; Goodyear, 2002; Brown, Collins and Duguid, 1989; Jonassen and Tessmer, 1999; Wenger, 2000). A new book by Etienne Wenger and colleagues, *Cultivating Communities of Practice* (Wenger, McDermott and Snyder, 2002), has a chapter applying their ideas to what they call 'distributed communities'. Martyn Sloman's recent book (Sloman, 2001) is good for exploring the challenges of online learning in corporate environments.

Engagement theory

From engagement theory comes the key idea that students must be engaged with other people – not just computer programs – as well as in meaningful tasks, in order for successful learning activities to take place (Kearsley and Shneiderman, 1998). Teams of learners (the 'participants' of this book) should work together on projects that are stretching and have application outside the learning time itself. This means that the activities need to be rooted in real-world experience.

Deep and surface learning

One way of considering learning is through surface and deep approaches. Deeper learning is demonstrated by the learners' ability to explain a topic to others, to apply it and consider related theories. The deeper learner will also display more 'engagement' around the topic and the learning experience. In other words, deeper learning is related to more active engagement, shallower learning to more passive responses to learning opportunities and environments (Biggs, 1999). So we can conclude that an active, more problem-based approach encourages online participants to adopt deeper approaches to a topic.

Reflection

The role of 'learning to learn' – reflection on activity, questioning previously held knowledge and developing a more strategic approach to study – is increasingly seen as important to lifelong learning approaches (Sharples, 2000). The importance of reflection goes back to the educationalist Dewey's early writing but there has been increased interest in researching and using reflective processes in adult teaching in the past 20 years (Bengtsson, 1995; Moon, 2000). In 1983 Schön pointed out that people change their everyday practice by having reflective 'conversations' with themselves and with other people. As a result of considering experience in this way they reinterpret or reframe their understandings of the experience. They may take action based on the reframing and, after further reflection, reinterpret the experience. Schön also argued that through reflection, a practitioner could surface and critique understandings that have grown up around a specialized or professional practice and make sense of them for him- or herself.

E-tivities can attempt to tap into and promote these notions (Salmon, 2002b).

Teaching strategies

Prosser and Trigwell (1998) distinguish two main pedagogical approaches: teacher focused and student focused. Teacher-focused strategies typically deploy transmission theories of teaching with the focus on what the *teacher* does. Student-focused strategies encourage the learners to change their view of the world and are based on what the *students* do. Learner-centredness draws heavily on the notion of the construction of knowledge, which emphasizes the key importance of the social process to learning. Peter Goodyear's excellent chapter in *Networked Learning* provides an underpinning and overview of the psychological areas (Goodyear, 2002).

Biggs (1999b) offers us a way forward for learner-centred learning. He suggests giving learners autonomy and control of the choice of their subject matter, learning methods and pace of study. The implication for learner-centred pedagogy is that the learner should be given the opportunity to process information, solve problems and make decisions. Project-based learning approaches have been one outcome (Blumenfeld, 1991). E-tivities are a safe way of introducing more learner-centred approaches, using the online environment.

E-moderating

Essentially, learning is a way of interacting with the world. As we learn, our conceptions of phenomena change and we see the world differently. The acquisition of information does not itself bring about a change but the way we structure and think about that information does (Biggs, 1999a). This means that each time an e-tivity is offered, it is essential to ensure that participants are given opportunities to structure the variety of contributions and that the e-moderator makes certain that they are left with some kind of plenary or summary. The role of the e-moderator in creating and developing learning through computer-mediated conferencing (CMC) is critically important, as Chapter 3 illustrates.

The impact of disciplines

The word discipline is derived from the Latin 'disco' (which means 'I learn' – not 'I dance'!) (Cybenko, 2000). Disciplines affect the way we think about methods of teaching and research. There are historical legacies framed by disciplines at every level of education, but especially in universities (Cuban, 2001). Disciplines strongly influence our professional identities and what information and know-ledge we think is valid and important. Despite changes in membership and dominant paradigms, the discipline itself continues often with its 'basic assumptions and approaches relatively intact for generations' (McDermott, 1999: 108). Most educational institutions are based on disciplines, and the 'going to college' experience is therefore bound up with perpetuating and promoting the discipline base. Even if we challenge the accepted ideas or ways of practice (as online educational provision has, for example, in the university communities through-out the world), we are still part of the inherited and transmitted wisdom of that community. The discussion on knowledge generation in Chapter 2 shows that each learner enters a territory already occupied by others. Typically we want participants to enter into the usual way of thinking for our discipline, and, in a corporate environment, the special aspects of our industry, our corporate mission and tacit ideas of how our organization or institution works. Therefore, e-tivities need to tap into the special aspects of each discipline or context in order to be authentic.

Computer-mediated conferencing, communication and media

Information technology has inspired the vision of widespread information sharing (Grudin, 1994). Research and work on computer-mediated conferencing and online discussion groups spans many years and predates the growth of the Internet, for example from Professor Robin Mason and her colleagues in the Institute of Educational Technology (IET) at the Open University (OU) (Mason, 2001; Mason and Weller, 2000). The ideas that individuals are part of rich social networks that can be promoted and harnessed in the service of group learning can be explored through the ideas of Brown and Duguid (2000). Theoretical and practical issues around computer-mediated conferencing include those of the role of critical thinking, legitimate discourse and challenges to assumptions and beliefs. Vivien Hodgson's recent chapter is a good place to start (Hodgson, 2002).

In my view, Diana Laurillard's book is still one of the best for exploring the advantages and disadvantages and uses of different kinds of media for teaching and learning purposes (Laurillard, 1993).

References

Ash, C and Bacsich, P (2002) The costs of networked learning, in *Networked Learning: Perspectives and issues*, eds C Steeples and C Jones, Springer-Verlag, London

Belbin, RM (1981) *Management Teams: Why they succeed or fail*, Butterworth Heinemann, Oxford, and [online] http://www.belbin.com/belbin%20team-roles.htm

Bengtsson, J (1995) What is reflection? On reflection in the teaching profession and teacher education, *Teachers and Teaching: Theory and Practice*, **1** (1), pp 23–32

Biggs, J (1999a) What the student does: teaching for enhanced learning, *Higher Education Research and Development*, **18** (1), pp 57–75

Biggs, J (1999b) *Teaching for Quality Learning at University*, SRHE and Open University Press, Buckingham

Blumenfeld, P (1991) Motivating project based learning: sustaining the doing, supporting the learning. *Educational Psychologist,* **26**, pp 369–98

Breen, R, Lindsay, R, Jenkins, A and Smith, P (2001) The role of information and communication technologies in a university learning environment, *Studies in Higher Education*, **26** (1), pp 95–113

Brown, J S, Collins, A and Duguid, P (1989) Situated cognition and the culture of learning, *Educational Researcher,* **18** (1), pp 32–41

Brown, J S and Duguid, P (2000) *The Social Life of Information*, Harvard Business School Press, Boston, MA

Carroll, J and Appleton, J (2001) *Plagiarism: A good practice guide*, Oxford Brookes University on behalf of Joint Information Systems Committee (JISC); [online] http://www.jisc.ac.uk/pub01/brookes.pdf

Churchill, E F, Snowdon, S N and Munro, A J (2001) *Collaborative Virtual Environments*, Springer-Verlag, London

Claxton, G (1997) *Hare Brain Tortoise Mind*, Fourth Estate, London

Cook, S D N and Brown, J S (1999) Bridging epistemologies: the generative dance between organizational knowledge and organizational knowing, *Organization Science*, **10** (4), pp 381–400

Covey, S R (1999) *Seven Habits of Highly Effective People*, Simon & Schuster, London and New York

Croucher, J (1996) *Exam Scams*, Allen & Unwin, St Leonard's, NSW

Crystal, D (2001) *Language and the Internet*, Cambridge University Press, Cambridge

Csikszentmihalyi, M and Csikszentmihalyi, I S (1988) *Optimal Experience: Psychological studies of flow in consciousness*, Cambridge University Press, Cambridge

Cuban, L (2001) *Oversold and Underused: Computers in the classroom*, Harvard University Press, Cambridge, MA

Cybenko, G (2000) The death of disciplines, *Computing in Science and Engineering*, March/April, pp 2–3

Darby, J (2002) Networked learning in higher education: the mule in the barn, in *Networked Learning: Perspectives and issues*, eds C Steeples and C Jones, Springer-Verlag, London

Duffy, T M and Cunningham, D J (1996) Constructivism: implications for the design and delivery of instruction, in *Handbook of Research for Educational Communications and Technology*, ed D H Jonassen, Macmillan, New York

Ehrmann, S C (2001) Emerging models of online collaborative learning: can distance enhance quality? *Educational Technology*, September–October.

Feather, N (1982) *Expectations and Actions*, Erlbaum, Hillsdale, NJ

Feenberg, A (1989) The written word, in *Mindweave: Communication, Computers and Distance Education*, eds R D Mason and A R Kaye, Pergamon, Oxford

Fox, S (2002) Studying networked learning: some implications from socially situation learning theory and actor network theory, in *Networked Learning: Perspectives and issues*, eds C Steeples and C Jones, Springer-Verlag, London

Gammon, S and Lawrence, L (2000) Using leisure experiences in the educational process, *Proceedings of Meeting of Minds*, Manchester Metropolitan University; [online] http://www.ilam.co.uk/downloads/minds/sgll1.pdf

Ghani, J A and Deshpande, S P (1995) Task characteristics and the experience of optimal flow in human computer interaction, *British Journal of Psychology*, **28**, pp 381–91

Gibbs, G (1992) *Improving the Quality of Student Learning*, Technical and Education Services, London

Goleman, D (1996) *Emotional Intelligence*, Bloomsbury Publishing, London

Goodfellow, R, Lea, M, Gonzalez, F and Mason, R (2001) Opportunity and e-quality: intercultural and linguistic issues in global online learning, *Distance Education*, **22** (5), pp 65–84

Goodyear, P (2002) Psychological foundations for networked learning, in *Networked Learning: Perspectives and issues*, eds C Steeples and C Jones, Springer-Verlag, London

Grossman, D (2002) *Be My Knife*, Bloomsbury, London

Grudin, J (1994) Computer-supported cooperative work: work, its history and participation, *IEEE Computer*, **27** (5), pp 19–26

Hodgson, V (2002) Issues for democracy and social identity in computer mediated communication and networked learning, in *Networked Learning: Perspectives and issues*, eds C Steeples and C Jones, Springer-Verlag, London

Honey, P and Mumford, A (1986) *Using Your Learning Styles*, Maidenhead, Honey

Hung, D W L and Wong, A F L (2000) Activity theory as a framework for project work in learning environments, *Educational Technology*, March–April, pp 33–37

Jasinski, M (2001) E-games: improvisation through open platform design: challenges for workplaces, colleges and universities, Southern Cross University, NSW [online] http://www.scu.edu/au/schools/sawd/moconf/

Jasinski, M and Thiagarajan, S (2000) Virtual games for real learning: learning online with serious fun, *Educational Technology*, **40** (4), pp 61–63

Jonassen, D H and M Tessmer (1999) *Learning with Technology: A constructivist perspective*, Prentice-Hall, London

Kearsley, G (2000) *Online Education: Learning and teaching in cyberspace*, Wadsworth/ Thomson Learning, Belmont, CA

Kearsley, G and Shneiderman, B (1998) Engagement theory: a framework for technology-based teaching and learning, *Educational Technology*, September/ October, pp 20–37

Knowles, M (1985) *Androgogy in Action*, Jossey-Bass, London

Laurillard, D (1993) *Rethinking University Teaching: A framework for the effective use of educational technology*, Routledge, London

Lauzon, A (2000) Situating cognition and crossing borders: resisting the hegemony of mediated education, *British Journal of Educational Technology*, **30** (3), pp 261–76

MacGilchrist, B, Myers K and Reed, J (1997) *The Intelligent School*, Paul Chapman Publishing, London

Mason, R (2001) Effective facilitation of online learning: the Open University experience, in *Teaching and Learning Online: Pedagogies for new technologies*, ed J Stephenson, Kogan Page, London

Mason, R and Weller, M (2000) Factors affecting students' satisfaction on a web course, *Australian Journal of Educational Technology*, **2** (1); [online] http://cleo.murdoch.edu.au/ajet16/mason.html

Mayes, J, Dineeen, F, McKendree J and Lee, J (2002) Learning from watching others learn, in *Networked Learning: Perspectives and issues*, eds C Steeples and C Jones, Springer-Verlag, London

McAteer, E, Tolmie, A, Crook, C, Macleod, H and Musselbrook, K (2002) Learning networks and the issues of communication skills, in *Networked Learning: Perspectives and issues*, eds C Steeples and C Jones, Springer-Verlag, London

McClelland, D C (1985) *Human Motivation*, Cambridge University Press, New York

McConnell, D (1999) *Implementing Computer Supported Learning*, Kogan Page, London

McDermott, R (1999) Why information technology inspired but cannot deliver knowledge management, *California Management Review*, **41** (4), pp 103–17

Mills, A C (2000) Creating web-based, multimedia, and interactive course for distance learning, *Computers in Nursing*, **18** (3), pp 125–31

Moon, J (2000) [accessed 7 May 2002] Reflection in higher education learning, PDP working paper 4 LTSN; [online] http://www.ltsn.ac.uk/genericcentre/projects/pdp/working-papers.

Morgan, G (1993) *Imaginization*, Sage, London

Osland, J. S and Bird, A. (2000) Beyond sophisticated stereotyping: cultural sense-making in context, *Academy of Management Executive*, **14** (1), pp. 65-79

Pitt, M. J (2001) How do you cope with cheating and plagiarism? LTSN Engineering Seminar, 21 November; [online] http://www.pble.ac.uk/group-workshop-2001-11-21/pble-ltsn-martin-pitt-Cheata.doc.

Polanyi, M (1966) *The Tacit Dimension*, Doubleday, Garden City, NY

Polyani, M (1962) *Personal Knowledge: Towards a post-critical philosophy*, University of Chicago Press, Chicago

Prosser, M and Trigwell, K (1998) *Teaching for Learning in Higher Education*, Open University Press, Buckingham

Rose, A (1992) Framing our experience: research notes on reflective practice, *Adult Learning*, January, p 5

Rossen, E (2001) Trust in virtual teams, in *Proceedings of World Multiconference on Systemics, Cybernetics and Informatics*, Orlando, FL

Rowntree, D (1999) [accessed 7 May 2002] A new way with words in distance education; [online] http://www-iet.open.ac.uk/pp/D.G.F.Rowntree/words_in_de.htm

Rumble, G (2001) The costs and costing of networked learning, *Journal of Asynchronous Learning Networks*, **5** (2), pp 75–96

Salmon, G (2000a) *E-moderating: The key to teaching and learning online*, Kogan Page, London

Salmon, G (2000b) Computer mediated conferencing for management learning at the Open University, *Management Learning*, **31** (4), pp 491–502

Salmon, G (2001) So this is what it looks like from space? in *Proceedings of Online Education Conference*, Berlin, November

Salmon, G (2002a) Approaches to researching teaching and learning online, in *Networked Learning: Perspectives and issues*, eds C Steeples and C Jones, Springer-Verlag, London

Salmon, G (2002b) Mirror, mirror, on my screen. . . exploring online reflections, *The British Journal of Educational Technology*, **33** (4), pp 383–96

Sharples, M (2000) The design of personal mobile technologies for lifelong learning, *Computers and Education*, **34**, pp 177–93

Sloman, M (2001) *The E-learning Revolution*, CIPD, London

Sternberg, R J (1999) Intelligence as developing expertise, *Contemporary Educational Psychology*, **24**, pp 359–75

Tolmie, A and Boyle, A (2000) Factors influencing the success of computer-mediated communication (CMC) environments in university teaching: a review and a case study, *Computers and Education*, **34**, pp 120–40

Trehan, K and Reynolds, M (2001) Online collaborative assessment: power relations and critical learning, *Networked Learning: Perspectives and issues*, eds C Steeples and C Jones, Springer-Verlag, London

Tuckman, B W (1965) Developmental sequences in small groups, *Psychological Bulletin*, **63**, pp 384–99

Tuckman, B W and Jensen, M A C (1977) Stages of small group development revisited, *Group and Organizational Studies*, **2**, pp 419–27

Walker, R (2002) Marking Open University scripts electronically, in *Institute of Teaching and Learning*, East Anglia Members' Forum, Cambridge, May

Weick, K E (1995) *Sense Making in Organizations*, Sage, Thousand Oaks, CA

Wenger, E (2000) Communities of practice and social learning systems, *Organization*, **7** (2), pp 225–46

Wenger, E, McDermott, R and Snyder, W M (2002) *Cultivating Communities of Practice*, Harvard Business School Press, Boston, MA

Williams, W *et al* (2001) Facilitating cross-cultural online discussion groups: implications for practice, *Distance Education*, **22** (1), pp 151–67

Wiske, M S (1998) *Teaching for Understanding; Linking research and practice*, Jossey-Bass, San Francisco

Wood, H and Wood, D (1999) Help seeking, learning and contingent tutoring, *Computers and Education*, **33**, pp 153–69

Index